REVENGE
VIRGINS' VOWS
THE ANNUITY

Aleksander Fredro

REVENGE
[ZEMSTA]

VIRGINS' VOWS
[ŚLUBY PANIÉNSKIE]

THE ANNUITY
[DOZYWOCIE]

translated by Noel Clark

OBERON BOOKS
LONDON

WWW.OBERONBOOKS.COM

First published in 1993 by Oberon Books Ltd
521 Caledonian Road, London N7 9RH
Tel: +44 (0) 20 7607 3637 / Fax: +44 (0) 20 7607 3629
e-mail: info@oberonbooks.com
www.oberonbooks.com

Translation copyright © Noel Clark, 1993

Noel Clark is hereby identified as translator of these plays in
accordance with section 77 of the Copyright, Designs and Patents
Act 1988. The author has asserted his moral rights.

A catalogue record for this book is available from the British
Library.

PB ISBN: 978-0-94823-064-6

Printed and bound by Marston Book Services Limited.

Contents

Introduction   7

Revenge   15

Virgins' Vows   101

The Annuity   209

INTRODUCTION

Polish literature has flourished for more than five hundred years. Yet few Polish writers of the past are familiar to the world at large. Unless you happen to be Polish, the name of Count Aleksander Fredro, for example, would hardly leap to mind in a random roll-call of contributors to the great community chest of European drama. To his compatriots, who have this year [1993] been celebrating the bi-centenary of his birth, Fredro (1793-1876) is the "Father of Polish Comedy". Generations of Poles have studied his works at school and university. During the World War Two German occupation of Poland, when the theatre, like much else, was driven underground, Poles risked imprisonment and worse to attend clandestine performances of *Revenge* and *Virgins' Vows*. The quips, aphorisms and names of Fredro's characters have invaded colloquial speech and, to this day, his best-loved plays, including the three in this volume, feature regularly in the classic repertoire of Poland's leading theatres. The first half of 1992 alone saw eight new productions of Fredro comedies.

A learned authority on his work – Poland's most celebrated translator of foreign literature, Tadeusz Boy-Zelenski, who was executed by the Nazis in 1941, once wrote that, by remaining for the world "a great unknown", Fredro had merely shared the fate of all the best Polish writers. Certainly, the names, let alone the works of the 19th century Polish "immortals" – Mickiewicz, Slowacki and Krasinski – are all but forgotten these days, except by their compatriots and foreign specialists. It may be that the great Romantic dramas – conceived in anguish and written in exile – were too exclusively Polish in their inspiration to make an extensive impact on world literature. The artistic by-products of so grievous a national tragedy as the loss of sovereignty for 123 years by a once-major European power, swallowed whole in 1795 by Russia, Prussia and Austria, were possibly more than Poland's helpless friends abroad could bear to contemplate. The poetry of those great works, moreover, was often of a kind that seemed to defy translation.

Fredro's failure to win wider recognition is less easily understood, for Fredro was a mainstream European dramatist whose comedies are fun to read and even funnier on the stage. In his humorous portrayal of enduring human traits, he is potentially the most accessible of Poland's classic writers – far closer to us in time and thought than, say, Molière. If, thanks to geography and history, Polish tears have a certain exclusivity about them, the same need surely not apply to Polish laughter.

Throughout Fredro's long life, Poland was a dismembered and occupied country, shaken sporadically by bloody upheavals and savage repression. But Fredro, instead of writing tragedies abroad, wrote comedies at home. This he could do with an easy conscience – or so one might have thought – for he, alone of all the Polish literary "greats" of the period, had actually fought in the field for Poland's independence.

The third son of a nine-child family of noble though impoverished gentry, Fredro, aged sixteen, followed his two elder brothers into the army of the short-lived Duchy of Warsaw, set up by Napoleon. As an officer in a light cavalry regiment, who was later to serve on Napoleon's staff, Fredro was among 100,000 Poles who fought in the Grande Armée. He shared with them the exhilaration of the 1812 advance to Moscow and the appalling hardships of the winter retreat. Four-fifths of the Polish contingent perished and with them Poland's hopes of liberation in return for backing the French against the Russians.

Fredro, who not only won the highest Polish and French decorations for bravery, but survived a bout of typhus and escaped from Russian captivity, was later to describe army life as "the most practical, varied and alluring of all schools of experience." Among other things, it provided him with material for a classic autobiographical memoir in the manner of Sterne's *Tristram Shandy*.

By his own account, Fredro's early education was sketchy. While still in uniform, however, he began to display clear signs of the talent which was soon to win him national acclaim. His early Muse was mainly, though not entirely, patriotic. An explicitly pornographic play in rhyme, understandably not included in his collected works, is said to have been performed with delight by brother-officers.

Disillusioned by Napoleon's ultimate defeat and failure to free Poland, Fredro – still only twenty-two – resigned his commission and returned to the family estate near Lvov, in the so-called Austrian Partition. Pausing in Vienna on his way home from Paris, he met and fell in love with the Countess Zofia Skarbek, a young Polish noblewoman, unhappily married. It was thirteen years before the Countess, having obtained an annulment, was finally free to marry Fredro, who had meanwhile inherited his father's title and begun to make his name as a dramatist.

Fredro was an author who wrote when he felt like it, rather than a professional man of letters. As he later recalled in a typically modest couplet:

> I missed the army and grew bored at times;
> For want of anything to do, I took to rhymes.

In all, he produced some forty works for the stage, many of them full-length comedy satires on Polish life and manners – urban and rural – together with one-act farces, music-hall sketches, an operetta, poems, fables, stories and a volume of philosophical squibs. The latter help to confirm the playwright as a shrewd but good-humoured observer of the human condition, an advocate of the golden mean, a satirist with a sense of fun and an admirer of traditional Polish virtues: courage, loyalty, fairness and generosity to the vanquished foe. "When hatred is being forged," Fredro once wrote, "a demagogue pumps the bellows and the devil wields the hammer."

Virgins' Vows – generally regarded as his most accomplished comedy – and *The Annuity* reflect the author's awareness of the disabilities suffered by young women in a male-dominated society, though the fate of the militant Clara in *Virgins' Vows* suggests some ambivalence in Fredro's thinking on the matter. His favourite targets were the *nouveau riches* – especially those who had made money out of the Napoleonic wars. He also mocked the then current mania for aping foreign customs – English as well as French – likewise, the frivolity, prejudice, complacency and moral laxity which he had observed among the well-to-do in Paris, Vienna and in his own provincial capital, Lvov. Like

Waclaw, the hero of *Virgins' Vows*, Fredro in his youth was a keen frequenter of parties and balls to brighten the tedium of country life. In *Revenge* (see some of Papkin's speeches) and in *Virgins' Vows* (Albin), he also ridiculed the mannered rhetoric of earlier dramatists.

Audiences in all three zones of occupied Poland were charmed by the novelty of Fredro's brisk, sparkling verse, ingenious rhyme-schemes, everyday language and homely regionalisms. For the first time, theatre-goers, starved of light relief, were able to laugh at the antics and dilemmas of characters who were no longer mere replicas of French or Italian models, conversing in neo-classical alexandrines, but recognizably Polish. In Warsaw alone, the Czar's censors, disturbed by the subversive potential of the one-word title "*Revenge*", insisted that playbills advertising the comedy expand the title to "*Revenge over a Boundary Wall*" – a change which could only have enhanced the play's attraction for Polish theatre-goers by suggesting a political sub-text to a seemingly innocent social comedy, based on an actual property dispute.

Following the collapse of the November 1830 revolt against Czarist rule, hundreds of Polish insurgents were hanged and thousands deported to Siberia. It was during the years of deep national depression that Fredro's most popular comedies were staged: *Virgins' Vows* (1833), *Revenge* (1834), *The Annuity* (1835). Malicious critics, no doubt envious of Fredro's success, but ostensibly for patriotic reasons, mounted a campaign against him. In 1835 and later, Fredro was accused of indifference to the national cause and his comedies denounced as immoral, derivative and lacking in talent. Deeply wounded, Fredro refused to allow any more of his plays to be performed or published in his life-time. From 1842 to 1857, he even stopped writing – devoting himself instead, as an important local landowner and a member of the regional assembly, to public affairs.

In holding aloof from active subversion in what must have seemed to him a hopeless situation, Fredro was arguably a realist. He remained, however, a Polish patriot, writing or signing many outspoken protests to the authorities in Vienna, as well as campaigning for the abolition of censorship and serfdom and for the recognition of Polish as the official language of the judiciary. In 1852, after being denounced as the author of a subversive, unsigned poem, he was tried and narrowly escaped being convicted of treason by the Austrians.

In a poem called "*Pro Memoria*", written when he was seventy-eight, by which time he had long since been "rehabilitated", a medallion struck in his honour and his genius celebrated with a gala performance of *Virgins' Vows*, Fredro looked back on these events:

> Silence alone seemed called for . . . . nothing less!
> So I stayed silent . . . fifteen years . . then, none the worse,
> I felt the old, mad urge to scribble verse!
> How through life's mazes, unnumbered paths meander!
> You can't foresee the outcome as you wander:
> Despite directions and a thread to follow,
> You find a gendarme, where you seek Apollo!
> So, to this day, I file what I create,
> Distrustful of their praise: it's come too late!
> This aide-memoire events long past recalls,
> So that I'll not be booed too loudly –
>
> > > When the curtain falls!

Though his later plays, published posthumously, have their admirers, they mostly lack the verve, wit and spontaneity of his early work. Like Polish dramatists before him, Fredro was influenced by Molière and Goldoni. His style is nevertheless his own. One Polish critic has described Fredro's brand of gentle satire as "free from Molière's bile and Gogol's brutality." Another credits him with having saved Poland from all-embracing melancholy. Without Fredro, it has been suggested, Poland might never have evolved a national comic tradition which, in our own century, has produced satirists of international repute such as Slawomir Mrozek and the late Witold Gombrowicz – the arch-debunker of "Polishness".

Now that Poland, after another period of enforced isolation, has resumed her rightful place in the mainstream of western culture, while we ourselves edge closer to our continental neighbours, this may be a good time to remind ourselves, with Fredro's help, of our common literary heritage and values shared.

Previously published translations of Fredro comedies – all of them in prose – have mainly been the work of American academics (the most recent and notable, Professor Harold B. Segel: *The Major Comedies of Aleksander Fredro*, Princeton University Press, 1969). However, an unpublished prose version of *Sluby Panienskie*, entitled *Maidens' Vows*, by the late Monica Gardner – a British author renowned for her efforts to popularise Polish literature and history – was performed in 1935 by a student drama society from Cambridge in a barn-theatre in Shere, Surrey. In a witty article, extolling this unique event, a Polish reviewer who was present, commented wryly that another Fredro comedy, *Pan Jowialski* (a satire on complacency and over-optimism) might have been even more to the taste of the English audience. Four years later, Poland was again invaded by her neighbours.

Although Fredro wrote many of his plays in prose, his choice of rhyming verse for those in this volume was deliberate. In trying now to re-introduce Fredro in colour, so to speak, rather than black-and-white, I hope a gain in fidelity to the spirit of his work will outweigh the sacrifice of literal precision, where dictates of metre and rhyme have prevailed.

I am grateful to Agnieszka Kreczmar of Warsaw – a gifted translator of English and American poetry into Polish – for volunteering to compare my translations in typescript, line by line with the original, in a last-minute hunt for "howlers" – and for alerting me in time! My thanks are also due to: Dr Maria Danilewicz Zielinska, Professor Jerzy Peterkiewicz, Dr Gerald Stone, Jan Repa, Jan Krok-Paszkowski, Boleslaw Taborski, Zbigniew Blazynski, Wieslaw Toporowski, Dr Zdzislaw Jagodzinski and staff of the London Polish Library; to Jolanta Mach who, as President of the Lodz branch of the Polish Literary Translators' Association, invited me to Poland (with the support of Lodz City Council and the British Council) to lecture on my Fredro translations – and, not least, to Gordon House, Executive Producer of BBC World Service Drama, who skilfully directed the first broadcast performances of Fredro in English. For all shortcomings in the translation, I alone am to blame – not the above-mentioned, whose interest and enthusiasm kept me going. Finally, for their support in introducing Fredro to a wider public, my thanks to the Arts Council of Great Britain – also to Hanna Mausch, Director of the Polish Cultural Institute in London and to Karol Drozd, the former Director.

NOTE: Some Fredro characters have names which could be translated after a fashion, e.g. *Dyndalski* (*Dither*), *Milczek* (*Taciturn*). I have preferred to leave them in Polish, for this, after all, is Fredro – not Sheridan.

NOEL CLARK [1993]

REVENGE
[ZEMSTA]

This translation of *Revenge*, adapted for radio by Anthony
Vivis and Tinch Minter, was first broadcast by the BBC World
Service in June 1987. The cast, in order of speaking, was as
follows:

SQUIRE	Rowland Davies
DYNDALSKI (butler to the Squire)	Richard Durden
PAPKIN (a soldier of Fortune)	Nigel Lambert
WIDOW ANNA	Jennifer Piercey
WACLAW (son of Milczek)	Mark Payton
CLARA (niece of the Squire)	Elaine Claxton
SMIGALSKI (servant in the Squire's house)	Tim Reynolds
NOTARY MILCZEK	Garard Green
COOK, MASONS, GROOMS, etc.	

ACT ONE

SCENE ONE

A room in the SQUIRE's castle, doors left, right and centre. Tables, chairs, etc. English guitar hanging on the wall. SQUIRE, in a zhupan (three-quarter length coat, part of nobleman's costume), without a belt but wearing a nightcap, seated at table right, spectacles on his nose, studying documents. DYNDALSKI, the butler, stands behind the table, slightly to the rear, hands behind his back.

SQUIRE: *(As though talking to himself.)*
                   A worthwhile match in every sense!
                   Forests, fertile land – her charms
                   Into the bargain – handsome rents!
                   Fine wife she'd make – with three good farms!

DYNDALSKI: Nice widow!

SQUIRE: Not just *nice*! A beauty!
                   (Arranging his papers.)
                   What about food? Go on, do you duty!
                   (Exit DYNDALSKI.)
                   Am I to starve to death with waiting?

                   DYNDALSKI meets liveried servant at the door carrying tray with small tureen of soup, plate, bread, etc., which he takes from him and returns. Fastens napkin round SQUIRE's neck and serves his soup without interrupting flow of conversation.

                   No point in procrastinating!
                   Clara's my ward: related to her,
                   No-one's better placed to woo her …
                   Snag is – Clara's young and frisky
                   Fall in love today, maybe –
                   Tomorrow – who can guarantee?

DYNDALSKI: *(Refilling his plate.)*

	Nobody in his right mind would!
	You must admit –
SQUIRE:	*(Turning towards him.)*

It might be risky
To sacrifice my bachelorhood
And see some –
(Pounds the table.)

Lightning strike him dead!
He'll have a good long wait ahead!
(Short silence, reaches for plate.)
Though Clara's fairly well-to-do –
The widow Anna's got much more …
I'll start by knocking at her door!
(Brief pause.)
She's staying here as Clara's guest –
The pair being distant kith and kin –
To me, the whole thing would appear –

DYNDALSKI: Someone…well…more…she hopes to win …

SQUIRE: *(Snorting with laughter.)*

Someone more … what? she hopes to win!?
Oh, Dyndalski, devil take you!
What a suggestion! … "hopes to win"!
Bah! You'd have me die of laughter!
Hopes? What *more* could she be after?
(Still eating, after a pause.)
She's still quite young, but she's got sense:
A widow has experience!
She knows just where to draw the line:
No time for dandies, fops or balls –
Shenanigans at carnivals –
(Short pause.)
I'm not, I grant you, in my prime:
Contrariwise, not all that old!

DYNDALSKI: *(Pauses, irresolute.)*

	Well –
SQUIRE:	*(Offended.)*
	You, yourself, if truth be told –
DYNDALSKI:	My age –
SQUIRE:	*(As though to end the conversation.)*
	You'll see! Just give me time!
DYNDALSKI:	*(Scratching behind his ear.)*
	Forgive me, Squire, for mentioning this –
SQUIRE:	Eh?
DYNDALSKI:	There's more to marriage than a kiss!
	Between ourselves, sir, you've got gout!
SQUIRE:	*(Obviously displeased.)*
	From time to time – a modest bout –
DYNDALSKI:	The gripes –
SQUIRE:	– that's when I've drunk too much!
DYNDALSKI:	And what about those shooting pains?
SQUIRE:	You're talking nonsense! Use your brains!
	Such trifling ills don't signify.
	Who knows what *she's* got? Matters such
	Are meet for God alone – and why
	Should anyone ask questions till –
	As man and wife, we split the bill!

Enter PAPKIN, dressed in French fashion. Sword, breeches, calf-length boots, kiss-curl and pigtail, three-cornered hat, pistols in shoulder-holsters. PAPKIN always speaks very fast.

PAPKIN:	God bless your Honour, and good cheer!
	Obeying your command post-haste,
	Horse after horse, to get me here,
	I quite wore out! The way we raced!
	My brand-new fly turned over! It's
	Scattered along the route in bits!
SQUIRE:	Papkin, my friend, I'll bet you wandered

	The whole way here on shank's mare
	And in some gambling-den, you squandered
	The cash I gave you for the fare!
PAPKIN:	*(Drawing pistol.)*
	Now, look Squire – I would have you know –
SQUIRE:	What?
PAPKIN:	I've been shooting!
DYNDALSKI:	*(Aside, on his way out.)* At a crow!
PAPKIN:	Where, at whom – I cannot say!
	It wasn't cards, though – that I swear –
	Which kept me late a fraction.
	Now was it sleep! Believe me, pray!
	A shot put each one out of action –
SQUIRE:	A swat – more like it!
PAPKIN:	What?
SQUIRE:	Gnats? Flies?
PAPKIN:	I know you think I'm telling you lies!
SQUIRE:	I wasn't born yesterday!
PAPKIN:	What's this I see? A breakfast-tray?
SQUIRE:	Breakfast indeed!
PAPKIN:	It isn't right:
	Six days and nights and not an hour
	I stopped to rest or snatch a bite!
SQUIRE:	Then eat and listen –
PAPKIN:	That's the way!
	(Sits down opposite SQUIRE and talks as if to himself.)
	Crackshot I am! Ne'er known to fail!
SQUIRE:	What's known is that I've got the power
	To have your goodself clapped in jail
	For trifles, not quite past and done!
PAPKIN:	*(Frightened.)*
	In jail? What for?

SQUIRE: Why, just for fun!

PAPKIN: Oh, find some other pastime, do!

SQUIRE: Fear not, I only mention it
                So that, my friend, you call to mind –
                Before your orders are assigned –
                What you owe me – and I owe you!

PAPKIN: Ask what you like! I'll see it through
                Sit any mount, nor turn a hair!
                As horseman, I'm without a peer!
                Break in a stallion? I don't care!
                Wild as a boar? Just let me near!
                They're meek as new-born lambs, I swear –
                Confronted by this cavalier!

SQUIRE: A pox on you!

PAPKIN: Now, listen Squire!
                I'd leapt to horse – was on my way.
                When, suddenly, this fight broke out,
                Occasioning me some delay.
                I'll tell you how it came about.

SQUIRE: Look!

PAPKIN: There I was, just riding out:
                A manly figure, braided hair,
                Chin up, with my commanding stare,
                The traitor sex to terrify!

SQUIRE: Listen!

PAPKIN: Presently! Don't shout!
                A Greek princess came driving by –
                Creature divine! Superbly wrought!
                (The sight of me makes girls distraught!)
                I looked her way; she ogled me!
                She'd fallen for me, I could see;
                She'd just called out – et cetera – when,
                The Prince – a tiger – grouped his men –

SQUIRE: *(Pounds the table; PAPKIN jumps up on chair.)*

Be quiet, can't you?

PAPKIN: Easy, Squire!

SQUIRE: You've got a wicked tongue, you rake!
Not just a babbler, but a liar!

PAPKIN: Oh, come sir! That's too much to take!
If I, like you, upon my soul,
Let passion rage beyond control –
(*Clasps hilt of sword.*)
Why, Artemis, my trusty sword –
(*Anticipating SQUIRE pounding table again.*)
Speak up, Squire, if you want a word!

SQUIRE: (After a brief pause.)
Clara's father – now the late –
Bought this castle and estate –

PAPKIN: Pah! My father owned a dozen!

SQUIRE: (Strikes the table and continues.)
Here we live like owls – with staff.
Alas, the castle's other half
Belongs to fiend in human guise:
Milczek, the Notary, by name:
Mild-mannered, sweet, with downcast eyes,
But with a demon in his soul!

PAPKIN: As neighbours, though, you have to be –

SQUIRE: Unless by stratagem or ruse,
I'll never prise him from his hole!
From fights and tiffs no day is free –
Somehow, we simply must agree!
To write him letters I refuse;
To visit him – too great a risk;
He'd slip me poison on the sly;
I'm still too fond of life to die!
Things being what they are, I'm keen
To use you as a go-between.

PAPKIN: I kiss your feet in gratitude!

You do me too much honour, Squire …
But I, alas, am fierce and crude:
Not peace, but war, I would inspire.
Within my mother's womb I grew,
For deeds of knightly derring-do;
In swaddling-bands, an oath I swore,
Never to play ambassador.

SQUIRE: Papkin will do as he is told:
The Squire commands and he obeys!

PAPKIN: Hotheaded as I am – and bold –
I might cut short your neighbour's days!
Were I to shoot him in the head,
Make mince-meat of him, slice by slice,
Who'd be to blame when he was dead?
And who would have to pay the price?

SQUIRE: My conscience would take care of it!

PAPKIN: Consider –

SQUIRE: No! Enough's been said!
There's something else, my friend – to wit:
With Papkin's help – - I mean to wed!

PAPKIN: Fie!

SQUIRE: What's "Fie" supposed to mean?

PAPKIN: Fi-ne! I'm delighted! More than keen!
Just tell me how to win my spurs.
Am I to match-make for your grace?
To stroke some kitten till she purrs?
Or tame some saucy jade in furs?
Or, if she's married and oppressed –
Shall I sword-stitch the tyrant's breast?

SQUIRE: Damn you and your crazy prattle!

PAPKIN: You know my courage, Squire, in battle!

SQUIRE: Papkin, between ourselves, by Hades!
No offense – but truth be told –

As far as brain-power goes, then mine
Surpasses yours a thousand-fold!
(PAPKIN tries to interrupt. SQUIRE silences him with a gesture.)
But, as for sweetening the ladies –
Flirting, courtship, all that stuff,
Small talk, arty-crafty chat –
Sooner have my head chopped off!
It's quite beyond me all of that!
For eloquence, I count on you!

PAPKIN: Squire, she'll be yours, without ado!
I guarantee a happy sequel.
In such affairs I have no equal.
One look from me – and women fall;
My looks subdue them, one and all!
I'm off!

SQUIRE: Where to?

PAPKIN: I don't quite know –

SQUIRE: The widow!

PAPKIN: Ah, I see – quite so.

SQUIRE: Wait for her here!

PAPKIN: I'm standing by!
Give me an hour – and she'll comply!

SQUIRE: You'll see, I'll make it worth your while!
(Exit SQUIRE.)

PAPKIN: I know the Squire does things in style!
He's a volcano in eruption;
If Papkin didn't rein him in,
Heaven alone knows what disruption –
(Short pause for reflection.)
I'll not lose out … 'Twould be a sin!
We'll share the booty in this wise:
He'll have the widow for his prize –
A shade antique, if still quite fine –

But pretty Clara shall be mine!
For years, I've cherished the desire,
In her young heart to light a fire!
Long since, the pair of us, well-matched,
No end of Papkins might have hatched,
Had not the Squire, like an hiatus,
Always contrived to separate us!
(Pause.)
But I must make my presence known:
A song! Let music's soothing tone
The loved one's gentle ear rejoice –
I'm blest with an angelic voice!
(*Sings to guitar accompaniment.*)
Darling daughter, do I dream?
What's that whispering I hear?
It's my kitten lapping cream –
Go to sleep now, Mother dear!
Mother mine, it's the kitty-cat-cat –
The noise in my room – it's only that

Darling daughter, tell me pray,
What's that clattering by your bed?
Mother mine – the cat, I say,
Hunting mice; no cause for dread!
Mother mine, it's the kitty-cat-cat-
The noise in my room – it's only that!

Darling daughter, tell me true –
Has that kitten of yours got feet?
(Softly.)
Mother, if you only knew:
Silver spurs and garments neat!
Mother mine, it's the kitty-cat-cat-
The noise in my room – it's only that!

Enter WIDOW ANNA through door right.

WIDOW: I was saying that, for sure,

Is either Papkin – or, it's cats!

PAPKIN: Oh, Mistress Anna! Wit abounding,
In so generous a vein!
Demi-angel! Virtue's cynosure!
In all the hemisphere surrounding,
Peerless in love, grace, charm you stand!
My humble duty, pray, do not disdain,
Allow me, on your snow-white hand,
The homage of my lips to press!
(*Kisses her hand.*)
Your servant most devoted, may I say?

WIDOW: And might I ask what brings you here today?

PAPKIN: Tidings that fill us all with happiness!

WIDOW: Of what, pray?

PAPKIN: Your betrothal –

WIDOW: Mine?!

PAPKIN: One night, Lord Pembroke came to dine,
He and some gentlemen of note –
A dozen chamberlains or so –
Distinguished folk I chance to know.
Ladies were few, but they were choice!

WIDOW: Matchmaking?

PAPKIN: Word spread – and I quote:
The lovely Anna is to wed!
It's true, some doubted what was said
And looked to me for confirmation.
My lady – female divinity –
Though devilish jealous, nonetheless,
Under the table, pinched my knee,
And, close to tears, sought revelation:
Didn't I know the lady's choice?
That she should worry, Lord forfend!
So, for her ear, with lowered voice,
I whispered "She's to wed a friend."

26

WIDOW:	But who? His name, for pity's sake!
PAPKIN:	A choice unanimously praised – Could anyone exception take?
WIDOW:	(Aside.) I understand!
PAPKIN:	Polite and able, Someone of substance – upright, stable!
WIDOW:	*(Aside.)* The Squire has sent him, I'll be bound! He just blows in from miles away, Where I have languished many a day – The silly man - !
PAPKIN:	*(Aside.)* Oh, damn my eyes! She's all undone, she pants and sighs. I fear that she's misunderstood And thinks it's me – as if I would! What plague it is – torment untold – To turn the heads of young and old! She must be mad! This ogling must stop! It's gone beyond a laughing matter! As if I'd stoop for crumbs that drop, Unnoticed from a rich man's platter! Better end it, here and now … (*To WIDOW.*) So, to the Squire, felicitations I'll convey, if you'll allow.
WIDOW:	You mean that I'm to be his bride?
PAPKIN:	Why ask? Or are there grounds to doubt The rumours flying far and wide?
WIDOW:	So far – yes –
PAPKIN:	But truth will out And very soon – if you ask me!
WIDOW:	Why all this curiosity?

PAPKIN: What if the Squire, aflame with passion,
               By your beauty quite unmanned –
               Trembling with love, in courtly fashion,
               Fell at your feet and begged your hand?

WIDOW: Then my reply would cause delight!
               (Exit WIDOW by door, right.)

PAPKIN: In each of them, an evil sprite
               Sits waiting, wanton tricks to play!
               But bearing her response in mind –
               Let any wise man tell me, pray,
               If one good reason he can find
               Why Mistress Anna should aspire
               To holy wedlock with the Squire!
               (SQUIRE, now fully dressed, bursts in through door, left.)

SQUIRE: Papkin, what are you waiting for?
               My property has been attacked.
               The Notary's waging open war
               But I'm a neighbour who'll react!
               He'll see! I'll give the rogue what for.
               Look lively! Stir you stumps and fight!
               Get moving! Put the scum to flight!

PAPKIN: What happened?

SQUIRE: It's the boundary wall!
               Three masons working on repairs!
               His orders! How the scoundrel dares!
               The boundary wall! They're laying bricks!
               I'll scatter them, frustrate their tricks –
               I'll smash, destroy, demolish all!

PAPKIN: *(Sounding confused, repeats reluctantly.)*
               Smash? Destroy?

SQUIRE: You give your word?
               Rally our men! Defend the wall!
               And if no plea for peace is heard,

	Then drive them from the work by force!
	You're shivering?
PAPKIN:	With rage, of course!
	But stay a while, if so disposed,
	To hear an ode I've just composed!
SQUIRE:	What?
PAPKIN:	"Ode to peace" … I have it here!
	But if it's war he wants, I fear
	He'll not be chastened by the Muses!
SQUIRE:	*(Threatening.)*
	Stay, if you will – but!
	(Exit SQUIRE, followed by PAPKIN, hanging his head.)
PAPKIN:	They'll be bruises!

SCENE TWO

WACLAW and CLARA. The garden. A section of the wall is visible. From the lefthand side, as far as the middle, it's in a good state of repair. But there's a break in the centre and the rest is partially destroyed. The labourers are working on this part. On the left, set well back, a tower or the corner of the NOTARY's residence can be seen, complete with window. On the right, slightly farther forward, a similar corner of the SQUIRE's residence is in view. Front stage, left, a summer house.

	(Enter CLARA, crossing the stage. WACLAW, having crept in through a gap in the wall, takes cover behind the bricks and re-appears beside CLARA in the summer house.)
WACLAW:	Our dwellings are so close together –
	Hearts much closer still – and yet –
	In this world far apart they're set!
CLARA:	What new demands, like clouds foregather
	Casting a shadow on your smile?
	No boundary wall, nor regulation –
	Nothing, it seems, can cramp your style –

Not even Clara's adoration!

WACLAW: To glimpse you only now and then,
And suffer hours of torment when
Denied your eyes, denied your voice –
Should such a fate make man rejoice?

CLARA: Come, sweet, you've not so soon forgot
The words you spoke that day we walked
Among the cloisters while we talked?
You said – if I mistake me not –
"Just let me love you! Nothing more
My tears entreat you! To the skies,
Sustained by loving you, I'll soar –
And, godlike, dwell in Paradise!"

WACLAW: I didn't know what I was saying!

CLARA: "Love, then! I'll not object," said I.
At which, great eagerness displaying,
You clasped my hands and, with a sigh,
"Do you love *me*, my darling Clara?"
You asked, repeating the refrain –
Though, from my eyes, the truth was plain!

WACLAW: Who'd not have paid with half his days,
If once his soul might drink its fill
From your dear lips on which that phrase,
Hid by a smile, was absent still?

CLARA: So be it … finally, said I:
"I love you" … and with all my heart!
(Mimicking his ardour.)
"Oh, what delight and joy!" you cried,
"Thank heaven! Earth! The sun on high!"
Your wishes, having satisfied,
Nature, the poorer for her part,
Had nothing further to impart!

WACLAW: I'll not deny the fact that – then –
My cup was filled to overflowing …

30

	But shouldn't the gifts be greater when
	My love has steadily been growing?
CLARA:	Did you not say, your pleas renewing,
	My casement grille, so closely spaced,
	Would be the cause of your undoing?
	"Look how those stems are interlaced –
	How each flower leans towards the next?
	Why shouldn't we? On what pretext?
WACLAW:	Was I – frustrated in my will,
	Expected to embrace the grille?
CLARA:	Waclaw, I understand you well:
	Each day, this summer-house we visit –
	And almost always, truth to tell,
	You make of me some new – requisite!
	Joy of my life to you I owe –
	A mutual debt, as I would hope –
	But why is this love which you bestow
	So eager to extend its scope?
	Enough for me – I'm by your side;
	That, in itself, is bliss for me!
	Today, you're still dissatisfied –
	Though hiding your anxiety!
WACLAW:	I'm frightened by the here-and-now …
	We've done so little to secure
	Our own, or our love's future. How
	Can we make certain both endure?
	Your uncle's and my father's strife –
	Eternal bickering, altercation –
	Augur ill for married life!
	They threaten us with separation!
	We'll be cruelly torn apart
	Unless –
CLARA:	I know – but what to do?
	Can I prevent it, more than you?

WACLAW:	You must show a change of heart
	In what may seem a hopeless cause –
CLARA:	Go on!
WACLAW:	Well then, my sweet, because
	We love each other to excess,
	Intent on finding happiness,
	The pair of us must be agreed –
	Not only one – with utmost speed
	To end this hole-in-corner play:
	Stop frittering our lives away,
	Stop waking every day in dread
	Of bliss being blasted by despair!
CLARA:	What can we do?
WACLAW:	We must be wed!
CLARA:	You're mad! How could we be, and where?
WACLAW:	The choice is yours –
CLARA:	My uncle's rather –
	He does the choosing – and your father!
WACLAW:	But if the way is barred, confound it –
	We must find a way around it!
CLARA:	Waclaw, no! That, I can't face!
	My heart is yours and will be ever;
	Yours to command, but not disgrace!
WACLAW:	As man and wife, no need to hide!
CLARA:	Should we elope, all contact sever –
	Who'd know you'd wed your stolen bride?
	What's that commotion? Pounding feet –
	They're coming closer! Quick retreat!
WACLAW:	One word!
CLARA:	I've nothing more to say!
WACLAW:	Relent! Or I shall die this day!
CLARA:	*(With feeling, as though correcting him.)*
	We shall – if you wish, my love!

WACLAW:	Clara, darling – give it thought!
CLARA:	*(Jostles him off-stage, right.)*
	Waclaw, run! Or you'll be caught!
	(Exeunt. Enter PAPKIN, SMIGALSKI and other Retainers of the Squire, armed with cudgels. Later, SQUIRE and NOTARY at their respective windows.)
PAPKIN:	Good mason, may I please request –
	Politely, kindly, gently, sir –
	That you stop worik, for you've transgressed –
	Or something nasty will occur!
	(Short silence.)
	My dear good men, why sweat in vain?
	Hammers, plumb-lines, trowels you ply
	Most skilfully, with might and main –
	But, really, there's no reason why!
	Be off with you! … And go to hell!
	(No response.)
	This won't be easy – I can tell!
	These louts are deaf! They pay no heed,
	Whether I threaten them or plead …
	Come on, Smigalski, we're enough!
	Brace up and take their tools away!
	Easy does it! Not too rough!
	Let's make an end of it, I say!
	Don't be afraid! I'm right behind you!
	(SMIGALSKI and Retainers advance on the Masons. PAPKIN retreats round a corner of the house.)
SMIGALSKI:	Clear off!
NOTARY:	*(Speaking from his window.)*
	Stand fast! What *is* all this?
SMIGALSKI:	The Squire, my master's order 'tis:
	The wall must not be renovated!
SQUIRE:	*(Speaking from his window.)*
	That's my order and my right!

Go to it! Put the rogues to flight!

(SMIGALSKI steps forward. PAPKIN, who had emerged briefly, again hides round the corner of the house.)

NOTARY:	What right?
SQUIRE:	The deed of purchase stated None shall touch the boundary wall.
NOTARY:	Esteemed and worthy sir, I call That madness! Though the wall is shared, Hasn't it still to be repaired?
SQUIRE:	I'll patch it with corpses, then!
NOTARY:	*(Calling to the Masons.)* Complete the work with courage, men! Ignore his threats, like me! Keep cool!
SQUIRE:	So you want bloodshed?
NOTARY:	Listen, Squire – Dear friend and most respected neighbour: Stop acting like a brigand and a fool!
SQUIRE:	Have at them, lads, with stick for sabre!

(SMIGALSKI and his men advance to the wall and the Masons fall back, so that the actual skirmish is hidden by the wall itself.)

NOTARY:	Mason, I'll plead you defence! Fear not! Let the scoundrel try – If he's so keen to take offense! Good! Someone's head has caught a crack! Hammer everything that moves! Don't be frightened! That's the way! Let him fight! We'll fight him back! For this, I'll have him locked away, Where he'll see neither earth nor sky!
SQUIRE:	*(Shouting over his shoulder.)* My flintlock, quick! No more ado!

I'll singe the feathers of that cockatoo!
Quick!
(NOTARY shuts his window.)
       Ha! Given us the slip!
Smigalski, hand those louts a tip!
Half a crown – no make it one –
To compensate for damage done!
But stow their captured tools away:
That'll do nicely for today!

(SQUIRE shuts his window. Exeunt all. Then PAPKIN appears, and after a good look around to make sure the coast is clear, addresses the wall.)

PAPKIN: Vagabonds, rogues! Out of my sight!
I'll grind your bones to chicken-feed;
I'll not leave one man-jack upright –
A battle royal's just what I need!
How many are you? Not a soul?
Does none dare venture from his hole?
Cowards! Rats in human form –
At dawn, I'll take the place by storm!

(Enter WACLAW, approaching PAPKIN from behind.)

WACLAW: At dawn?
(PAPKIN doffs his hat.)
By rights, I'm homeward bound –
But if it is your solemn vow
To raise my quarters to the ground –
I'd sooner be made prisoner now!

PAPKIN: *(Replaces his hat aslant, sign of his recovering nerve.)*
You're crying "Pax"?

WACLAW: Yes, seize me, pray!

PAPKIN: You know my strength?

WACLAW: By ill-repute!

PAPKIN: You fear me?

35

WACLAW:	More than I can say!
PAPKIN:	You follow me?
WACLAW:	Without delay!
PAPKIN:	Who are you?
WACLAW:	I am – who I am!
PAPKIN:	Who's that?
WACLAW:	That is to say, I'm me!
PAPKIN:	*(Reaching for his pistol.)*
	Who's me? You're *what*? In heaven's name!
WACLAW:	My master's agent!
PAPKIN:	What? The Notary's man?
WACLAW:	The Notary's agent – yes, the same!
PAPKIN:	Ye gods! Believe it if you can!
	These gentry are no sooner landed,
	Than they run up a heap of debts
	And need an agent. To be candid,
	Hardly reason for surprise,
	If soon, we hear the agent's cries –
	"Fifty thousand for this lot?
	Did I hear fifty-five? … Or not?
	Twice and thrice, in vain, he tries.
	Like stone from sling, the owner flies!
	No twist of fortune could be subtler –
	The lord becomes his agent's butler!
	Let's go!
	(Aside.)
	Squire'll be convulsed with joy!
	He's bound to recognize my coup.
	The moment I present this boy,
	He'll give me Clara, as my due.
	Quick march, prisoner! No demur!
WACLAW:	Marching right behind you, sir!

END OF ACT ONE

ACT TWO

(The SQUIRE's room as for ACT ONE. SQUIRE seated at table. Enter PAPKIN, followed by WACLAW, who remains standing near the door. PAPKIN throws himself into a chair.)

PAPKIN: I'm exhausted, quite unmanned –
              Barely fit to walk, or stand!
              That was really quite some fight!
              Enemies to left and right!
              Drop of wine might help a little –
              I'm poleaxed – even drained of spittle!
              Sweat? By the bucketful, I shed it
              How I fought, you'd never credit!

SQUIRE: Had I not seen it!

PAPKIN: Without fear –
              A born leader –

SQUIRE: From the rear!

PAPKIN: What matter, from the rear or no?
              A brave knight terrifies the foe.

SQUIRE: You've got a nerve!

PAPKIN: Indeed I have!
              Believe me, nerve was what was needed:
              Without it, I'd have not succeeded.

SQUIRE: Papkin, I know you're telling lies!

PAPKIN: Just listen, this is quite a story!
              I planned to take the work-site by surprise,
              But leapt so high, I overshot the quarry,
              And there was I upon the other side –
              Hemmed in, surrounded, all escape denied
              By masons, labourers, grooms and flunkeys,
              Coachmen, postillions and such monkeys!
              You'd never guess what I did then:

37

I singled out two sturdy men
And grabbed the fellows by the hair,
Then twirled them briskly through the air!
Like threshing flails, dispersing chaff,
I used them on the Notary's staff.
Each time I swung my cudgels round,
Ten more defenders hit the ground!
The heap of bodies grew so tall,
It finished level with the wall,
Whereupon I opened either hand,
Stepped straight across and – here I stand!
What's still more –

SQUIRE: How you have the face!

PAPKIN: Astonishment's not out of place!
I took a prisoner and now aspire
To don my wreath of laurels, Squire!

SQUIRE: *(Catches sight of WACLAW.)*
What *is* all this?

PAPKIN: *(Mopping his brow.)*
      As you observe,
I've Milczek's agent in my thrall!

SQUIRE: Why? What purpose does that serve?

PAPKIN: I gather up all fruits that fall!

SQUIRE: *(To WACLAW.)*
Go home! Godspeed you on your way –
And tell your worthy Master, please:
Let him provoke me as he may,
I'll match his every ploy with ease!
Whatever he does, I'll make him pay!
Before he's time to wink an eye,
I'll blow his residence sky-high!
Be off with you, young man! Good-bye!

PAPKIN: You give your all in duty's name –
Fight like Achilles, talk like Cato –

	For what reward? Begrudged your fame
	And pushed aside – like cold potato!
WACLAW:	*(To SQUIRE.)*
	If I may make so bold with you,
	Permit me, Squire, a word or two.
	Your neighbour has aroused your fury,
	Sometimes standing in your path –
SQUIRE:	Sometimes? Always?
WACLAW:	But I'm sure he –
SQUIRE:	No, the reptile's earned my wrath!
WACLAW:	But could this quarrel not be mended?
	Given, both parties have offended?
	Why not forget what went before
	And harmony 'twixt friends restore?
SQUIRE:	Between the pair of us goodwill?
	Not till the sun above stands still –
	Not till the seven seas run dry,
	Will he and I see eye to eye!
WACLAW:	Perhaps in heat of passion, Squire,
	Too hastily, you speak your mind –
SQUIRE:	From pestilence, from war and fire,
	From that disgrace to humankind
	Who bows so low before all men –
	Good Lord, deliver us – Amen!
WACLAW:	Better bent low than ramrod-stiff!
SQUIRE:	Fiddlesticks!
WACLAW:	If –
SQUIRE:	There is no "if"!
WACLAW:	Don't banish hope, however slim!
SQUIRE:	Yes, banish hope! I'll not endure it!
	I want to hear not more of him –
	Nor of his –
	(Pointing ironically at WACLAW.)

Sermonizing curate!!
Take care, my friend, or on my oath,
I promise you, I'll crush you both!

(Exit SQUIRE through centre door, leaving PAPKIN and WACLAW.)

PAPKIN: The devil's on the rampage in that Squire!

WACLAW: Attempts to reconcile them are in vain.

PAPKIN: So much ado - all for so little gain!

WACLAW: As well try bring together wood and fire!

PAPKIN: The question now is, what are we to do?

WACLAW: You captured me, so I'm your prisoner still.

PAPKIN: Oh, fie on prisoners – nothing new!
Thousands have bowed to Papkin's will.
I've battled these ten years and more,
Seen springs and rivers red with gore;
At times, things looked four miles around
As though the land were scarlet sea.
For military valour, I'm renowned:
Medals and honours by the score –
Titles and gifts were heaped on me!
This playground skirmish can't compare –
Your freedom's neither here nor there!

WACLAW: I stay a prisoner, as I've told you!

PAPKIN: Of course, I've got the right to hold you,
But my behaviour's always handsome:
I'll settle for a modest ransom!

WACLAW: I must stay captured, I insist!

PAPKIN: My magnanimity's greater still!
You're free to go! You can't resist!
Contribute only what you will …

WACLAW: No, I'm your prisoner – stay I must!

PAPKIN: Squire won't agree – to my disgust!

WACLAW: Who captures me must keep me, too –

40

PAPKIN:	Poppycock! Be off with you!
	You're free to leave! Just disappear!
WACLAW:	I will not budge a step from here!
PAPKIN:	I'll use my gun! You see I'm armed –
WACLAW:	*(Speaking very calmly.)*
	I have my fists. I'm not alarmed …
PAPKIN:	*(Aside.)*
	What ails the man, for Heaven's sake?
	He's bent on trouble, no mistake!
	How'll I get rid of him unharmed?
	(To WACLAW.)
	God save you, but begone, I pray!
WACLAW:	I won't begone! I'm staying here!
PAPKIN:	This stubborn moth won't fly away!
WACLAW:	*(Holding out his purse.)*
	Look here, my friend – see what I hold?
PAPKIN:	It clinks … it jingles – -
WACLAW:	Gold!
PAPKIN:	Real gold?
WACLAW:	It could be yours –
PAPKIN:	Sir, take a chair!
WACLAW:	There is, of course, a quid pro quo!
PAPKIN:	The golden rule – it's only fair!
	What must I do, I'd like to know?
	My cash position's very tight:
	The interest which I draw by right
	I cosset with a lover's care –
	Somehow, my pockets, just the same,
	Are either full of holes or bare!
WACLAW:	Now, I love Clara –
PAPKIN:	*(Aside.)*
	That's your game!
WACLAW:	And so, I want to stay close by.

PAPKIN:	Bad news!
WACLAW:	*(Makes as though to put his purse away.)* How so?
PAPKIN:	*(Reaching out to restrain him.)* It could be worse! I only meant that, should you try, The Squire will surely be adverse!
WACLAW:	He mustn't know!
PAPKIN:	What if he guessed?
WACLAW:	Let him employ me –
PAPKIN:	Hard to fix –
WACLAW:	*(Rattling his gold.)* That's the start! You do the rest.
PAPKIN:	He'll give me hell for playing tricks!
WACLAW:	What matter?
PAPKIN:	Huh? Depends to whom – ? *(Shaking his head.)* An agent – what will Clara say?
WACLAW:	I'm Waclaw!
PAPKIN:	Milczek's son and heir?! Here? In the Squire's own sitting-room? You've put us both in danger's way! He'll flay the pair of us, I swear! *(WACLAW rattles his purse.)* They jingle nicely!
WACLAW:	Yours to spend, If I get taken on, my friend!
PAPKIN:	I'll do my best, but – *(Trying to grab the purse.)*
WACLAW:	*(Pushing his hand away.)* By and by – First, get this fixed inside your head, My watch-tower suits a marksman's eye:

42

	Aim, fire, bang – and Papkin's dead
	Should he be tempted to betray!
PAPKIN:	You can rely on me to play
	Discreetly! You'll not be misled.
	I won't be gulled by anyone!
	But, Waclaw, if you cherish me,
	I beg you not to load your gun!
WACLAW:	We're wasting time!
PAPKIN:	I'm off! Don't fret!

(Aside.)

For such a triumph, thank the Evil One …
By ever-deepening troubles I'm beset:
My prisoner turns out to be a rival;
Worse still, he threatens my survival!
Squire locks me up, or Waclaw fires a shot –
And Papkin's done for! Devil take the lot!

(Coming back from the door.)

	What of the purse?
WACLAW:	It's safe with me –
PAPKIN:	Our bargain?
WACLAW:	Safe beyond all doubt!

(Exit PAPKIN though centre door. Enter CLARA.)

CLARA:	For heaven's sake, what lunacy?
	Waclaw, what are you about?
	If time allowed, I would despair!
WACLAW:	What's happening? What's gone amiss?
CLARA:	How can you smile, despite all this?
	I overheard the whole affair!
	You want to stay here?
WACLAW:	Yes, indeed!
CLARA:	Have sense!
WACLAW:	It isn't sense I need!
	We know it's nothing but illusion,

That our two fates can be united,
Counting on sweet reason's sage collusion!
Why not forgo a path that's blighted,
And choose another way instead?
Towards the dawning gleam of hope,
Now brightening the dark ahead,
Let's march in search of wider scope!
We'll neither look to right nor left,
Each yawning precipice ignore –
With heads upraised, eyes fixed before,
Step bravely forward, as of right!
By constancy, along the route,
Sustained in our agreed pursuit –
Quarrels and setbacks we'll survive
And, one day – surely – we'll arrive!

CLARA: Well spoken! That's a better way;
We're getting nowhere, as you say.
You've convinced me: let's contrive!
It really makes much sounder sense
Than to elope – which we discussed.
But won't they see through your pretence?
Might Papkin not betray your trust?

WACLAW: Avert your eyes from the abyss!
And gaze instead into your heart –
And every fear, love will dismiss
And dire misgivings all depart!

CLARA: Then – stay! God bless your enterprise!
I accord you my permission!

WACLAW: That is a prize as dear to me
As life itself – on one condition:

CLARA: I know – my Uncle must agree …
We'll tackle him with Anna's help.
About the time the battle raged,
The pair of them became engaged.

A modest soul, by no means grand,
With fiery cheeks, she pledged her hand.
You'll win her round with greatest ease:
Just praise her – she's not hard to please!
Extol her virtue, wisdom, grace –
Her person, figure and her face.
The moment you have made your mark,
You'll have a job as Uncle's clerk –
And so, kept busy filling pages,
You can be in the house for ages!

WACLAW: Agent to clerk is scarce promotion!
Ill may come of false attire.
Never mind, I like the notion:
Honoured to assist the Squire!

CLARA: I'll run and tell her someone's waiting
With a plea. That's all I'll say;
(Giving him her hand.)
Cheer up! Our troubles are abating –
Happiness not far away!
(Exit CLARA by door right.)

WACLAW: An hour past, she was fit to faint –
Now she's a paragon of force:
Fearless, a creature of resource,
Sustained by *more* than hope. How quaint!
O fair sex, lovable and loving!
Your joys and sorrows, as they break,
Are swift as ripples on a lake –
Each following with scarce a pause –
Advancing as the last withdraws –
In the sunlight, wavelets blending,
Clear as crystal, never-ending!
We, proud masters of Creation –
Swept away, despite ourselves –
By their elusive animation,

Spend our lives, as chance gives rise,
Pursuing them like butterflies!
(Enter WIDOW ANNA by right-hand door.)

WIDOW: Where is this man? What does he seek?

WACLAW: *(Bowing very low.)*
I'm the intruder –

WIDOW: Young, I see!

WACLAW: *(Still in bowing position.)*
I come as supplicant, too meek
To raise my eyes immodestly.

WIDOW: Isn't it Waclaw?

WACLAW: Why! It's Anna!
I'm at a loss –

WIDOW: I feel quite weak!

WACLAW: Then you're the widow who'll bestow –

WIDOW: You'd no idea?

WACLAW: An hour ago –
(Aside.)
How do I play this? It's absurd!

WIDOW: My husband died. You hadn't heard?
God love his soul! He was my third –
Our union in the Spring was blessed;
Come Autumn, he was laid to rest!

WACLAW: Oh, now I think I do recall –

WIDOW: He breathed his last upon my breast –

WACLAW: His last? Oh yes – his last, of course!

WIDOW: My grief was dire! He was my all!
A husband's loss is pain profound,
But time drowns every woe, perforce.

WACLAW: Your late lamented husband drowned?

WIDOW: Who said so?

WACLAW: Oh, then, didn't he?
That's good – but, now I have to go!

WIDOW: *(Restraining him.)*
Your wits, your words are all at sea!
You could be mad, for all I know!

WACLAW: Could be –

WIDOW: *(With emotion.)*
Never mind your shyness –
Now you're caught, I'll keep your Highness!

WACLAW: That title, you must please forget!
See how I'm blushing, hot with shame
For folly that I much regret:
Neither the rank, nor yet the name,
Had Waclaw any right to claim!
For both were - -

WIDOW: What?

WACLAW: Imagination!

WIDOW: Everything?

WACLAW: Sheer fabrication!

WIDOW: You're not a Prince?

WACLAW: I never was!

WIDOW: But why, then, did you –

WACLAW: No real cause –
A student jape – a prank I played –
A pointless, wanton escapade –
Tomfoolery – but not a crime!

WIDOW: You said you loved me, at the time!

WACLAW: *(Aside.)*
Now I'm in a pretty pickle!

WIDOW: Why ever blush, if you're that fickle?
I waited! Then, a prey to mania –
I scoured the whole of Lithuania!
Of Prince Rodoslav – not a trace!
Nobody knew the name or face!

WACLAW: I was a youth –

WIDOW:	*(Sarcastic.)*
	"I was a youth!"
	And yet, pastmaster of your art!
WACLAW:	Oh, I don't know!
WIDOW:	But it's the truth!
WACLAW:	How so?
WIDOW:	As proved by your betrayal –
WACLAW:	If I have changed, is that surprising?
	Few love in perpetuity.
	If you condemn my faith as frail,
	What of *your* promiscuity?
	Close at hand, your line you cast:
	No lengthy wait to fuel desire –
	The lid scarce shut upon your last –
	You quickly captivate the Squire!
	And when the Squire has served his day,
	You'll make some other man your prey!
	I don't reproach you … what's the use?
	God give you joy as you philander –
	But grant at least, what fits the goose
	Is just as fitting for the gander!
	For, if my sentiments have changed,
	Were you, yourself, not first to fall?
	Treacheries have been exchanged –
	Or else no treachery at all!
WIDOW:	But I'm a widow, Waclaw dear!
WACLAW:	And I'm a married man – or near!
WIDOW:	Who are you? Such a well-known face!
WACLAW:	Milczek's the name –
WIDOW:	The Notary's son?!
	Here? In this house?
WACLAW:	I'm out of place …
WIDOW:	I'm terror-stricken! Quite undone!

	My heart throbs – mist before the eyes – If Squire should take you by surprise, A rival find?
WACLAW:	Not that, for sure!
WIDOW:	No good pretending you're so pure! Not long ago, you seemed intent On seeing me, if I'd consent … What did you want?
WACLAW:	Damned if I know! High time I went! Good-bye, farewell!
WIDOW:	*(Holding him back.)* You haven't changed much, I can tell! Stay where you are!
WACLAW:	*(Aside.)* Papkin, old son, I'm captured now – and no mistake!
WIDOW:	I've always loved you! I would shun A hundred princes for your sake! To my rooms make your way by stealth; Once there, in safety, you can hide. I'll stake my life to guard your health – And your defence shall be my pride!
	(Enter CLARA by right-hand door)
WACLAW:	*(Agonised look, at sight of CLARA.)* Oh!
CLARA:	*(Merrily.)* What's wrong?
WIDOW:	It's just –
WACLAW:	All's well!
CLARA:	*(To WIDOW.)* What does he want?
WIDOW:	*(Aside.)* What can I say?

CLARA: *(Aside.)*
She's on his side, if looks can tell!
(Aloud.)
Or am I not to know it, pray?

WACLAW: Why, oh, why?

WIDOW: His supplication
Is of such weight it will require
Before I act, some – cognition.
Meanwhile, on no account disclose
His present lodging to the Squire!
A little later, I'll explain.

WACLAW: *(Sotto voce to WIDOW.)*
I'm going!

WIDOW: *(Sotto voce to WACLAW.)*
No, you must remain!
(Aloud.)
Forgive us if we now withdraw:
A complex case, involving law –
A document I've got to scan –
(Kisses CLARA's forehead.)
Clara, my dear – about this man –
Remember, quiet as a mouse!

CLARA: No one will know he's in the house!

WIDOW: A careless word could spell defeat;
I'll tell you all, next time we meet.

(Exit WIDOW, with nod to WACLAW who follows her with head bowed, through door on right.)

CLARA: *(Alone.)*
What could be funnier, if perchance,
The one misled should now mislead?
To see him, with submissive glance,
Entreat her in his hour of need!
From laughing I could scarce refrain –
But steady, miss, it's early yet!

The victory is not yet won.
We've started well – that much is plain.
But still, the battle 's far from done!

(Enter PAPKIN.)

PAPKIN: As in the far Arabian sand,
When Phoebus' golden rain descends,
And lily sears with scorching brand,
So that her pure white head she bends –
When, garnered in the heavens blue,
To bring new life to withered brow,
Regenerating drops of dew
The famished flower with strength endow –
So your sweet presence here has been –
With equi-active, equi-potent charm –
A honey-flowing source of joy serene
(Bows low.)
To cheer your humble servant, ma'am!
For I, myself, might well have faded,
Had not your looks recovery aided.
Let now the gods controlling fate
Permit me to reciprocate:
And be – before Time's reaper calls –
Your flame – and then, the dew that falls!
(Bowing low.)

CLARA: *(Ironical throughout, with low curtsey.)*
That one so rich in words and deeds
Should woo a maiden thus, must needs
Be termed a noble privilege!
But, these days, it's by no means rare
For ardent men with worthless pledge
The wedding-garland to prepare:
It's hard to know quite whom to trust!

PAPKIN: How can you doubt me, heavens above!
But, if you do, then Papkin must

51

Swear some great oath to prove his love!

CLARA: As to love – no problem there!
But will the future match the start?
Once passion cools, an oath's no use!

PAPKIN: Oh, in the flower-bed of my heart,
Would that I might your seed induce
To germinate, put forth a shoot –
And there, take ever-lasting root!

CLARA: In bygone days, a gallant knight,
With victory laurels his by right,
From many a bloody battle dour,
Before declaring his amour,
His lady's honour would uphold,
By jousting in a tourney bold.
And when, with lance, and by main force,
Ten challengers he did unhorse,
At last, triumphantly, he'd wheel
And at the loved one's bidding kneel –
From her dear hand the prize receive,
And only then would he beg leave
To love her and her favour wear:
Joust for his love and break a lance –
Live for his love – or die perchance!

PAPKIN: Surely, my costume and my sword
Proclaim me to be Mars's ward –
A man whose ever-chivalrous role
Has shuttled him from pole to pole!
Let Artemis, my trusty blade,
Whose steel the whole wide world dismays –
As 'twere a sponge – confused and gory –
Let it, in these more modern days,
Inspire your trust, proclaim my glory!
(With increasing ardour.)
High on cliff-top's stony crown,

Where cannon weigh the ramparts down,
And bayonets raise a wall of iron –
With pikes and sabres for a vault –
There fights proud Papkin, like a lion:
God's champion, Devil's axe-man in assault!
Moan, groan, hack, slash! Around him – death!
Men crying "Mercy!" with their dying
breath;
Maidens wring their hands in woe;
Mothers, children shriek with dread;
His sword-arm decimates the foe
And those alive are shortly dead!
(CLARA snorts with laughter.)
Forgive this blood-and-thunder tale
Of chivalry and virtues male!
No stranger I, to glory's portals!
I crave your leave to take my place
Among the ranks of happy mortals,
Whose talisman is lovely Clara's face.

CLARA: I grant it – -

PAPKIN: *(On his knees.)*

                And I pledge my troth.

CLARA: Now, years of trial to test your oath!
Obedience must be demonstrated,
Courage, constancy and duty!

PAPKIN: Beloved monarch, Queen of beauty,
Ornament of all created:
Bid me "Jump into that fire!"
And, in the flames, your Papkin will expire!
(Rises to his feet.)

CLARA: Less drastic shall be my request –
No jewel of chivalry's estate
Shall victim fall to such a fate!
But, I repeat, I mean to test

Obedience and steadfastness.
Your courage likewise shall be tried …

PAPKIN: To prove each one shall be my pride!

CLARA: As for obedience, I decree
That you stay silent half a year –

PAPKIN: Say nothing?

CLARA: Not a word, my dear!
To test your steadfastness – let's see –
Perhaps a bread-and-water diet – -

PAPKIN: Pray not too long – it makes me nervous!

CLARA: One year, six days –

PAPKIN: Condemned to death!

(Bowing.)

But, ever faithful – at your service!

CLARA: Now courage: here's the shibboleth!
Let him who will give proof of it:
In some far land, can still be found
A poisonous monster, world-renowned,
That holds the bravest men appalled:
A crocodile, I *think* it's called.
Go, catch it, for I'd love to see
This terrifying prodigy!
I'm curious beyond all measure:
You'll not deny me such a pleasure!
That is my will and my command.
He who obeys and does not falter
Will surely lead me to the altar:
On him, I shall bestow my hand!

(Exit CLARA through door on right.)

PAPKIN: *(After a long pause.)*
A crrrrrocodile!
(With irony.)
Not hard to find!

What an idea, for heaven's sake!
If girls have crocodiles to mind,
Their appetite for thrills to slake,
Then, by some modish trend insidious,
The beautiful's become the hideous!
There was a time when maids contrary,
Lovers might with sighs entreat:
"What I'd like is a canary!"
Now, they tell you bluntly: "Sweet,
Unless you are prepared to lose me,
Catch a crocodile to amuse me!"
(Brief pause.)
Silence and fasting? Fiddlesticks!
There'll be no sentries there to check.
It's just that monster put me in a fix.
Papkin, for sure, won't risk his neck!
*(PAPKIN moves towards door right and meets
WACLAW rushing in.)*
Ha!

WACLAW: What?

PAPKIN: Nothing!

WACLAW: *(Throwing him the purse.)*

                                Quiet, or else!

PAPKIN: I know …

            (Exit WACLAW. Brief pause, PAPKIN CONTINUES.)

                    I know not – go or stay?
What's the cash for, either way?
I've no idea! At least, it's gold
And it was good of him to pay me.
For all I *do* know, though, the Squire
May well be in the mood to slay me!
Nor will Waclaw hold his fire
If I should give the game away –
But what I don't know, can't foresee –

Is whether, at the end of play,
The Squire won't make an end of me!
I know, I don't know … Options pall!
Either a sword or else, a ball!
But, it's been said, I understand:
Blessed is he with cash in hand!

(Enter SQUIRE through door on the left.)

SQUIRE: Congratulate me on success!
I am engaged, if you've not heard:
At long last and without regress,
The Widow's given me her word!

PAPKIN: I well know how you came to win it:
Who, but myself, was instrumental?

SQUIRE: Who but yourself? Now, wait a minute!
Fact is, *you* were incidental!
(Looks round to check nobody's listening.)
I chanced upon a time propitious;
It was child's play – quite delicious!
She threw me a flirtatious wink
And as I hastened to the brink,
Led me on with due decorum –
This and that, then tit for tat –
But, just as I was edging closer:
Suddenly – smack! We disengaged –
(In high good humour.)
With womanly modesty outraged,
Her cheeks flushed red as cochineal;
Embarrassment brought me to heel.
But, as I beat a swift retreat,
Relying on my nimble feet,
I heard the Widow cry in haste:
"Stay, Matthew, don't dash off like that!
Your will be done! It's to my taste!
Submissively, I bow my head!

	Here, take this ring – and let's be wed!"
PAPKIN:	Well, I'll be damned! She played that well!
SQUIRE:	*(Angrily.)*
	You watch your tongue – or go to hell!
	(He points towards the door.)
PAPKIN:	As ever, prone to anger, Squire!
	Our squabbles would indeed be dire,
	Without my soothing influence!
	Let's turn to things of consequence,
	If you'll allow –
SQUIRE:	That's my advice!
PAPKIN:	The Notary's young man you met –
	I mention it lest I forget –
	Is keen to enter your employ.
	Would you, by chance, accept the boy?
	Loyal, hard-working he would be,
	But more than that –
	(Sotto voce.)
	reputedly,
	He takes his liquor like a man!
SQUIRE:	Drunk or sober, cuts no ice!
	Won't have him here, at any price!
	You don't think I'd be first in line
	To raid the Notary's rubbish-tip!
	But if, the Notary by design,
	Forbade the youth to flee his grip –
	I might employ him out of spite.
	You'll soon know if he's jumping ship …
	I've had fresh thoughts how best to fight!
	Arising from this morning's sport
	And sundry damage to the wall,
	Our neighbour's taking me to court –
	So *I* shall let my second call!
	Your job, my challenge to convey:

Tell him, we'll meet at four today –
In Blackwood glade with sabres drawn!
(Softly.)
One ear is all I'll need to crop;
He'll run before the other's shorn!

PAPKIN: You'd better write –

SQUIRE: Good heavens, no!
A second calls and he explains!
The job is one that calls for brains!

PAPKIN: But, Squire, I really must confess,
My recent illness left me less
Than brilliant –

SQUIRE: That may well be so!

PAPKIN: Well then –

SQUIRE: Stop quibbling – just go!

PAPKIN: But Squire, by all that's great and good,
Don't send poor Papkin to his doom!
Before you lop, the Notary would
Have time to put me in my tomb!
You said this morning, did you not?
"He'd slip me poison on the sly;
I'm still too fond of life to die!"

SQUIRE: On the sly? He never would –

PAPKIN: Your very words!

SQUIRE: As if he could
Put paid to you before my eyes!

PAPKIN: The devil sleeps not –

SQUIRE: Rubbish! Lies!

PAPKIN: *(Gestures to indicate being hanged.)*
What if he did – ?

SQUIRE: *(Threatening voice.)*
Just let him try!
I'd beat the scoundrel black and blue!

PAPKIN: What good, if Papkin's past all hope –
               Already dangling from a rope?

SQUIRE: *(Coaxingly.)*
               Come, Papkin, don't disgrace yourself!
               You'll not refuse a wad of pelf?

               *(SQUIRE gives PAPKIN a kiss on the forehead and
               exits by door left. PAPKIN, grimacing and shaking
               his head, leaves by centre door.)*

               END OF ACT TWO

ACT THREE

(Room in the Notary's part of the castle. NOTARY, seated at desk. Two MASONS standing in the doorway.)

NOTARY: Come, Master Mason, don't be shy!
    I'll write it down; you testify.
    In these hard times, a welcome onus;
    They trounced you, true, but that's a bonus!
    We'll make them pay for every blow –
    They beat you soundly – as we know!

MASON: Well, not exactly –

NOTARY: Yes, they did!
    Battered, I'd say!

MASON: No, not quite!

NOTARY: What else were they about, ye gods?
    Quite clearly spoiling for a fight!

MASON: Well, yes, there were some jabs and prods –

MASON 2:   Who wants to, can complain – not I!

NOTARY: A jab's not tickle? Do I lie?

MASON: Indeed not!

NOTARY: Battery and assault!

MASON: I see!

NOTARY: It's not the cudgel's fault
    If all your bones aren't shattered:
    A beaten mason's one who's battered!
    Don't you agree?

MASON: You put it well …
    Beaten is …

NOTARY: Battered; it's the same!
    A clear-cut case and they're to blame!

MASON: Could be, I s'pose … Bit hard to tell …

NOTARY: *(Writing.)*

You're crippled, aren't you?

MASON: No, not me!

NOTARY: Cross your heart?

MASON: Oh, no!

NOTARY: Any yet –

You've scratches ... why?

MASON: *(After whispered discussion with MASON 2.)*

We'll have to see ...

NOTARY: Scratches are wounds, don't you forget!

So you were wounded and you bled!

MASON: Well ... so to speak ...

NOTARY: A wound – quite so!

No matter whether deep or no.

How did it happen?

MASON: ... Like you said ...

NOTARY: They crippled you?

MASON: Ah, that was it!

NOTARY: To have a wound is not a whit

Less grave then being mutilated –

And since a scratch is much the same –

We can on oath quite fairly claim

That you have suffered injury,

Resulting in your penury!

MASON: That's something new!

NOTARY: It must be stated;

Since you couldn't ply your trade,

I couldn't pay you, I'm afraid –

(Continues writing.)

There! – crippled – and, as we have said,

In consequence deprived of bread –

With mother, wife and children – four?

MASON: No children –

MASON 2:	Single! Wish I had –
NOTARY:	You haven't? Well, no need to fret –
	You still might have – you're young, as yet!
MASON:	Yes –
MASON 2:	True enough!
NOTARY:	*(Stops writing.)*
	That's that! Not bad!
	And now you'll witness how the Squire,
	Intent on murder, opened fire –
	How the old buffer aimed at me
	And shot.
MASON:	He did? I didn't see.
NOTARY:	Called for his gun –
MASON 2:	I didn't hear!
MASON:	He shouted for his flintlock – true –
	He said – to shoot a cockatoo!
NOTARY:	A cockatoo? A cockatoo?
	No, that's enough! Leave it there!
	No matter! Somebody will swear;
	Of witnesses the world's not short!
	Come here! Still closer! You must sign.
	Your mark - a cross will do in court!
	Michael Kafar – there, that's fine!
	Now, Matthew Mientus – good – that's all!
	Those crosses are worth cash, you'll see.
	Our precious Squire will burst with gall!
MASON:	Be pardon, it occurs to me –
	A bill, long due, requires attention –
NOTARY:	Don't fret, the Squire will meet the cost –
MASON:	This goes way back; I'm loathe to mention –
NOTARY:	Don't worry; nothing will be lost –
MASON:	A job I did –

62

NOTARY: *(Pushing him towards the door.)*
        Good-bye! Godspeed!
        You know the house, so there's no need –

MASON: Bills here get paid, so people say –

NOTARY: *(Still pushing him.)*
        Or must I help you on your way?!

MASON: *(In the doorway.)*
        Look!   After all –

NOTARY: *(Closing door behind them.)*
        Farewell, good-day!
    (Returning.)
    I'll eat my hat and pawn my belt
    If I don't smoke that ruffian out!
    I'll make the weight of justice felt –
    With plenty to appeal about!
    According to my information,
    From private sources in the know,
    The old Squire's present jubilation
    Will shortly be transformed to woe!

    (Enter WACLAW.)
    A well-timed visit, son! Good-day!
    We've something that should be discussed:
    (Sits down and motions his son to a chair.)
    The many virtues you display
    Encourage my implicit trust
    That, like your father, you will tread,
    Lifelong, the paths of righteousness,
    Never by evil thoughts misled,
    Nor those who'd tempt you to disgress.
    That said, my heart is filled with joy –
    Since, *quandoquidem*, death is due –
    Knowing that I'll survive in you!
    (Wipes tear from his eye.)
    Trials, persecution, toil, my boy –

Peripeteia I've endured,
Submissively for your sweet sake,
To the Almighty's will inured;
So I, my son, for what I'm worth,
In your well-being have a stake:
Your welfare's my last wish on earth!

WACLAW: Proofs of paternal love – though rare –
Are dear to me beyond compare!

NOTARY: In you, my final hopes reside –
Though foes, begrudging consolation,
Son from father would divide
Rejoicing in my consternation.
Satan iniquity prepares:
Your youth is set about with snares!

WACLAW: Sorry, I don't quite –

NOTARY: – understand?
The Squire's ward, Clara –

WACLAW: She's a pearl!
I love her!

NOTARY: You've been underhand!

WACLAW: If I declined to name the girl,
The reason was my wish that, first,
Ill-will 'twixt neighbours be dispersed!

NOTARY: Between the Squire and me, O Lord!
Who – more than I – could wish accord –
Peaceful, God-fearing, to the core?

WACLAW: May I wed Clara with your blessing?

NOTARY: Certainly not! No point in pressing!
As I love peace, the Squire wants war!

WACLAW: But, is it Clara who's to blame,
Each time her uncle catches flame?

NOTARY: Be that as may be, there'll be strife!
Where you're concerned, it's all the same –

	For you shall wed a different wife!
WACLAW:	Oh, father, that's a cruel decision!
NOTARY:	One that will suffer no revision!
WACLAW:	But you declared my happiness
	Your only wish on earth, no less!
NOTARY:	God be my witness! True, as stated –
WACLAW:	I love her!
NOTARY:	*(With a smile.)*
	So it would appear!
WACLAW:	I'll die if we are separated!
NOTARY:	You can't deter me, so don't try it!
WACLAW:	I swear!
NOTARY:	Now that will do! Be quiet!
	Fate deals a hand to everyone –
	Therefore, let Heaven's will be done!
	But why so staunch in your reaction?
	What of that earlier attraction?
	You're tongue-tied? Why – ?
	(Ironically.)
	A shock, I suppose,
	To find out how much the old man knows!
WACLAW:	When I was young –
NOTARY:	Anna, by name –
	Remember your eternal flame?
	You loved her; you'd have walked through fire!
	Well, Anna's staying with the Squire …
WACLAW:	*(Quickly.)*
	She's his fiancée, you're aware?
NOTARY:	That, my boy, I'd never credit –
	Unless herself it was, that said it!
WACLAW:	But hasn't she? It's true, I swear!
NOTARY:	I questioned her on this affair:
	If God permits, I understand,

	She's ready to give you her hand!
WACLAW:	But I'm not ready to receive it!
NOTARY:	Obedient son, I can't believe it!
	I've signed a marriage settlement,
	Wherein it states, without dissent:
	One hundred thousand must be paid
	If either breaks the promise made.
WACLAW:	Is not my happiness worth more –
NOTARY:	With her as wife, that's catered for!
WACLAW:	I'd sooner die than do your will …
	Why, if the Squire were living still
	He'd shoot the pair of us at sight!
NOTARY:	(With customary phlegm.)
	Then he'd be hanged – and serve him right!
	Let Heaven's will on earth be done,
	Acclaimed by all, opposed by none!
WACLAW:	Father!
NOTARY:	Son!
WACLAW:	A knife of steel
	You've plunged into my luckless heart!
NOTARY:	No evil that's not good in part!
WACLAW:	Please change your mind!
NOTARY:	A vain appeal!
WACLAW:	(Throwing himself at his father's feet.)
	Have pity!
NOTARY:	Pity, you request?
	Behold my tears!
WACLAW:	(Standing up again.)
	Then you'll relent?
NOTARY:	Alas, my son, there's no repeal!
WACLAW:	Despair will drive me mad! Repent!
NOTARY:	I'm weeping; let my tears suffice!
	Virtue, my son's, an edifice –

A seed which, nutured with intent –
(Exit WACLAW. NOTARY, alone, speaks after pause.)
Too young to listen to advice!
(After pause.)
How that Squire persuaded her –
A tempting widow, suave, urbane –
Such a reptile to prefer
It's beyond me to explain …
If so, I'm convinced we'll find
She's more than pleased to change her mind.
(Throwing back his shoulders.)
Youth has its function to fulfil,
Yet old men may be sprightly still!
Once that Squire becomes aware
That he's been jilted! Holy smoke!
What he won't do! I hardly dare –
He could be flattened by a stroke!
Let Heaven's will on earth be done –
Acclaimed by all, opposed by none!
(Enter PAPKIN, advancing timorously.)

PAPKIN: May I come in?

NOTARY: Indeed, please do!

PAPKIN: A gentleman and Notary,
In one person to behold
At home, is for the likes of me,
A privilege and joy untold!
I hope I've not mistaken you?

NOTARY: No, quite correct! Your humble servant!
And whom – my pleasure is not less –
Have I the honour to address?

PAPKIN: *(Aside.)*
So meek a worthy! It's absurd!
He backs away with every word!
I needn't have been so concerned!

67

(Boldly.)

I am Papkin!

(NOTARY, bowing, points to chair in centre of room. PAPKIN looks attentively at NOTARY who, as always, stands motionless with arms folded on his chest. PAPKIN, aside.)

      … looks to me

As though I have an easy task!

(Aloud, sprawling in armchair.)

Lion of the North and, since you ask,

An officer, much decorated –

(Showing off medal ribbons.)

Here and there – and all well-earned!

Wise in council, bold in strife –

A knight, ill-tuned to peaceful life.

Swedish and Muselman battalions,

Saxons, Spaniards and Italians –

Have all met Artemis, my blade!

My sword-arm's strength, they've all assayed.

Need I go on? To sum it up:

The whole world know this name of mine!

Now, brother, what about some wine?

NOTARY: *(Hesitates briefly, then, aside.)*

Nemo sapiens, nisi patiens

As the proverb rightly states:

Wise is he who sits and waits!

(Takes bottle from under the table where it's been hidden by a cloth, holds it up to the light, pours one small glass and hands it to PAPKIN.)

PAPKIN: *(Aside.)*

You lily-livered, would-be gent!

The Squire's command I shall convey –

But, while the sun shine, let's make hay!

(Puts on his hat and drinks.)

Ugh! Beastly!

(Drinks again.)
              Foul!

NOTARY: So self-assured!

PAPKIN: Oh! This stuff's atrocious, brother!
            Are you sure you have no other?

NOTARY: I'm sorry if it's not matured –

PAPKIN: So much for gentry! Did you ever?
            (Showing contempt.)
            Live in the country, sow and reap,
            Grumble, grizzle, scold and fuss!
            You call this wine, it's scandalous!
            *(Goes to the table and helps himself to some more
            wine. NOTARY, unmoved, follows him with his
            eyes.)*
            One wonders where this swill was bottled –
            Fearsome colour … It's all mottled!
            And he begs pardon for the slop!
            Don't bow and scrape, my buckwheat baron!
            Run and fetch a better drop!

NOTARY: My dear, good sir –

PAPKIN: It's muddy, vile!
            Dregs, Notary, dregs! Is that your style?

NOTARY: *(Aside.)*
            He'd try the patience of a paragon!
            But – let Heaven's will be done!

PAPKIN: Visit any cellar of mine –
            Taste the whole world's choicest wine –
            A hundred barrels in a row –
            If you could find a crop this coarse,
            You'd win a saddle – and a horse!

NOTARY: *(Bowing.)*
            Forgive me asking, if I may –
            As yet, I've no means of telling –
            What brings a son of Mars this way

	To kindly grace my humble dwelling?
PAPKIN:	*(Lounging in chair beside table.)*
	You want to know?
NOTARY:	That's what I meant –
PAPKIN:	I'm here, you rogue, to represent
	No less a noble than the Squire,
	Whose castle, earlier today,
	By your retainers – men you hire –
	Was set upon in bold affray.
	Louts – the like of him they serve –
	Who dared invade the Squire's preserve!
NOTARY:	A shade more quietly, if you will,
	My hearing's quite effective still!
PAPKIN:	I always speak as I prefer.
NOTARY:	But I've a splitting headache, sir!
PAPKIN:	*(More loudly still.)*
	If someone's ears can't stand the din,
	Or someone else's headpiece ails,
	Stentorian voices can't begin
	To ape the song of nightingales!
NOTARY:	*(Gently.)*
	I think, since I've my servants near,
	I'll order your defenestration!
	(PAPKIN gets up slowly while the NOTARY is speaking and removes his hat.)
	It's quite a way for you to fall!
PAPKIN:	Don't trouble, please!
NOTARY:	I've but to call –
	Hey, there!
PAPKIN:	You've really no occasion –
NOTARY:	You'll float as lightly as a feather!
	(Shouting to servants off-stage.)
	Four of you, wait outside the door!

PAPKIN:	Surely when neighbours talk together,
	Protocol they may ignore?
NOTARY:	Now I'll gladly hear you out!
	(Pushes him back into his chair.)
	Get on with what you have to say …
	(Sits down facing PAPKIN, very close.)
	What was it that you came about?
	(Looking PAPKIN straight in the eye.)
PAPKIN:	I can see you're quite distraught;
	I'd really not idea, good sir,
	Your hearing was so finely wrought!
	Just warn me if perchance I err,
	Enunciating too distinctly!
NOTARY:	Just tell me quickly and succinctly!
PAPKIN:	*(Very softly.)*
	The fact is the Squire requests –
NOTARY:	Eh?
PAPKIN:	Louder? *(NOTARY nods and PAPKIN continues.)*
	that the Squire requests –
	Or rather that the Squire suggests –
	That, so to speak, one might put paid
	To disagreements which have made –
	(Unable to avoid the NOTARY's gaze, PAPKIN becomes still more confused.)
	It's as I say, yes – which have made
	For disagreement … Who'd deny
	That it's … or could at least conduce …
	(Turns away, then aside.)
	He's fixed me with the Evil Eye –
	My tongue has withered – it's no use!
NOTARY:	It's quite beyond me to conceive
	The point of such complexity!
PAPKIN:	*(Standing up.)*
	It was – forgive me, I believe,

Your wine – a trifle strong for me –
The least articulate of men –
(More quietly.)
Are those four guards still on parade?

NOTARY: My dear sir, let me help you then:
What is it that my neighbour wants?

PAPKIN: His emissary's a bit –

NOTARY: Afraid?
He need fear nothing for the nonce …

PAPKIN: His envoy bears the Squire's request
That you, sir, meet him about four
To put the issue to the test,
With sabres drawn, in Blackwood glade.

NOTARY: *(Ironical.)*
The old Squire's still a dashing blade!

PAPKIN: *(Plucking up courage; louder voice.)*
Indeed – and instances are legion
Of how unerring are his blows!
The Squire's renowned throughtout the region
For notching many a high-born nose!
There's still –

NOTARY: Less noise, for goodness' sake!

PAPKIN: *(Glancing towards the door.)*
Yes, indeed! More quietly then,
The Squire's polite request I make,
Adding my own – that's if I may –
For your rejoinder: yea or nay.

NOTARY: My answer he shall have on paper,
Though the timing's far from clear.
If he's to wed, will not this caper … ?

PAPKIN: *(More boldly.)*
Shouldn't really interfere!
The ring at morn; at four the duel –

72

NOTARY:
A cup at eve; at night –
(Sweetly.)

Hush, pray!

PAPKIN:
Quiet of course!
(Aside.)

Oh, this is cruel!
Not a whisper! I would lay
The Devil led me into this!

NOTARY:
(Ironically.)

The Squire's quite sure of married bliss?

PAPKIN:
Yes, indeed! His turtle dove
Thrice daily swoons – and all for love!
The Squire, no less aflame than she,
Beams like a candle full upon her!
They'll make a perfect pair, your honour.
Stake my limbs, my hands and feet –
She'll be a faithful as she's sweet!

(Enter WIDOW ANNA.)

WIDOW:
My presence here beneath your roof,
As you requested and designed,
Should in itself be seen as proof
That – Notary, I've changed my mind!
I wasted no long hours, dear sir,
On futile meditation;
When one's decided, why defer
Decision's confirmation?
Nor did I pause to tell the Squire
That I'd decided to retire
Because his neighbour pleased me better!
As you will see, I've signed your letter,
And, at your bidding, here I stand –
(Proffering a folded sheet of paper.)
There's the original in your hand;
I'll keep a copy to ensure

	Our understanding will endure!
	Thus, jointly bound by process due,
	Your daughter-in-law embraces you!
NOTARY:	Lady most bountiful of love,
	Radiance floods me from above!
	Good fortune's golden argosy
	Has spread its mighty sails for me –
	Since willing and with good grace,
	Your precious heart has found a place
	For this most humble of my pleas!
	Yes, lady bountiful of love,
	Radiance floods me from above
	And, doubtless, on my progeny,
	Still greater brilliance shall be shed,
	Since, with blest magnanimity,
	You deign to share young Waclaw's bed!
	Will you now graciously consent –
	Here in my modest tenement –
	To let me offer you my own
	Assurance of goodwill eternal –
	Faithful service diurnal?
	To fall at your feet is all I crave –
	To be your footstool and your slave!

(Kisses her hand.)

PAPKIN:	*(Aside.)*
	Ye gods! What's this? I'll eat my hat!
	He's pinched the Squire's intended wife
	To make her Waclaw's bride for life!
	Just let the Squire get wind of that –
	He'll slit him open like – a sprat!
WIDOW:	Dear Notary, make no mistake:
	It wasn't just an itch for change
	That prompted me to make the break!
	To me, your son's by no means strange –

	We know each other – very well!
	Why should I not admit sincerely –
	I loved him and he loved me – dearly!
PAPKIN:	*(Claps his hands.)*
	Good lady, look this way!
WIDOW:	What? Why?
	Do I see Papkin?
PAPKIN:	That you do!
	I hoped you'd deign to catch my eye.
WIDOW:	*(To NOTARY.)*
	You let this fellow call on you?
	(To PAPKIN.)
	Out of my sight!
PAPKIN:	*(With alacrity.)*
	I'm going!
NOTARY:	Wait!
PAPKIN:	I'm waiting!
NOTARY:	There's my answer still –
WIDOW:	It was this man's deceitful word
	That swayed my feeble, woman's will:
	Misled, reluctant – I concurred …
PAPKIN:	Me?
WIDOW:	Had fate not stooped to save,
	I'd have become the tyrant's slave!
PAPKIN:	*(To himself.)*
	Black day!
NOTARY:	*(To WIDOW.)*
	Let Heaven's will be done –
	Acclaimed by all, opposed by none!
	Since the Squire's not yet apprised,
	I think we might be well-advised
	If I included in my letter
	News of this turning for the better.

You, Mistress Anna, for you part,
Might well charge Papkin to impart
Your confirmation of the change;
He can recount what I'll explain.

PAPKIN: *(Aside.)*
The devil wants to get me slain!

NOTARY: That's for you, madam, to arrange;
While I withdraw to draft my brief!
(Exit NOTARY. PAPKIN's eyes follow him intently as he leaves the room.)

PAPKIN: This, madam, passes all belief!
Your conscience must be very strange!

NOTARY: *(Putting his head round the door.)*
Quietly!

PAPKIN: Ah, yes … I recall …
(Aside.)
That devil heard us through the wall!
(Quietly to the WIDOW.)
Madam, what is this you've done?
You'll get us slaughtered – every one!
No question! Don't you know the Squire?
He'll never stomach such disgrace.
Death he'll deal by sword and fire –
Make a shambles of your place –
Home reduced to dust and ash!
Let's escape! Let's make a dash!
(Peering round nervously and edging the WIDOW towards the door.)
I think you still don't realize
Into what peril you have strayed!
Hush! But for Artemis, my blade,
Whose strength deters – our swift demise –
Good Lord, protect us, hear our prayers!
Quick! Out the door and down the stairs!

76

WIDOW:	*(Tearing herself away.)*
	The way is clear –
PAPKIN:	It's not! I know!
	Four servants –
WIDOW:	As for my affairs:
	Bid the Squire for me "good morrow"
	Courtesy will ease the blow …
	Tell him also how my heart
	Is cruelly transpierced by sorrow
	At being forced this way to part –
	He mustn't think that I'm to blame!
PAPKIN:	Such balderdash, in heaven's name,
	The Squire will never hear from me!
	(Enter NOTARY.)
NOTARY:	Let noise, I beg!
PAPKIN:	I quite agree!
NOTARY:	My letter for the Squire's complete –
PAPKIN:	This envoy's job is fraught with danger!
NOTARY:	Godspeed!
PAPKIN:	*(Bowing.)*
	I am prostrate at your feet!
	So warm a welcome for a stranger!
	(Bows and ceremonious gestures by both.)
NOTARY:	Don't mention it!
PAPKIN:	Oh, but I must!
NOTARY:	*(Escorting him to the door.)*
	Most sincerely, at your service!
PAPKIN:	Please don't stir!
NOTARY:	But I entreat!
PAPKIN:	I beseech!
NOTARY:	Just to the door!
PAPKIN:	Can't allow –
NOTARY:	You'll see my four –

(Doors open to reveal Flunkeys.)

PAPKIN: Ceremony makes me nervous!

NOTARY: *(To Flunkeys.)*
Show this gentleman the way –

PAPKIN: Much obliged, but I'll not stray!

NOTARY: Look after him! He'll need a cane!
The stairs are dark; watch out, my son!

PAPKIN: Farewell, Godspeed – my thanks again!

(He bows, clears the threshold in one bound. Door closes, followed by clatter as of somebody falling downstairs. WIDOW, startled, moves towards the NOTARY.)

NOTARY: *(Walking away from the door.)*
Let Heaven's will on earth be done –
Acclaimed by all, opposed by none!

END OF ACT THREE

ACT FOUR

(Dining hall in the SQUIRE's home, with side-doors and a large door leading to the chapel. Tables for guests on both sides of the stage. Table on the right with ink-well and writing materials, bottle and two glasses. Festive garlands are being put up in the background. As curtain rises, DYNDALSKI is seen standing beside the SQUIRE, who is seated. DYNDALSKI is holding a pair of sabres while the SQUIRE examines a third, as he speaks the opening lines. SMIGALSKI and COOK are standing behind.)

SQUIRE: *(Sabre in hand.)*
      Time's getting on, Smigalski – so,
      Saddle the roan and off you go!
      Rush the invitations out –
      Don't forget what I want done!
      Tell them three times, every one:
      Tomorrow, at the Squire's request,
      They're welcome as his wedding-guest.
      Is that quite clear? Quick, on your way!
      (Exit SMIGALSKI.)
      Perelka, watch your step tomorrow!
      No elbow-bending, no wee drams!
      Or, mark my words, I'll roast your hams!
      Let's have a gourmet's paradise!
      No need to scrimp on this occasion:
      Bags of cinnamon, herbs and spice –
      A first-class banquet – hang the price!
      Perelka special – every dish!
      Figs, almonds, saffron with the fish:
      More than enough for everyone –
      Make sure you do this well, old son!

COOK: Sir, for the table – what device?
      Initials set in sugar-ice?

SQUIRE: M for Matthew; A for Anna:
            Heart above, "Long live" below;
            Spread around in tasteful manner!

COOK: Sir! You'll have a splendid show!
            (Exit COOK.)

SQUIRE: Where's Papkin? What's the man about?
            That fox, the Notary, in his lair,
            I know will take some smoking out –
            But I'll unearth him, that I swear,
            If, in his madness, he persists
            In stirring up some fresh to-do!

DYNDALSKI: Touching wood, in any case,
            The ablest swordsman in the lists
            Would get well tickled, tackling you!

SQUIRE: *(Exchanging one sable for another.)*
            And they've got mighty ticklish skins,
            Those learned doctors of the robe!
            Not one of them can stand the pace,
            However briskly he begins!

DYNDALSKI: Ha!

SQUIRE: *(Unsheathing sword.)*
            Mylady of Bar, I call this blade …
            She served me there and, in those days,
            At Slonim and Podhajce slew –
            Lomazy and Berdyczow, too!
            The world has changed in many ways:
            Bold youth, in battle unafraid,
            To older heads then still paid heed –
            As by the Lord Himself decreed;
            But things have changed a lot since then:
            The egg's now wiser than the hen!
            (Short pause.)
            A sturdy hilt, a blade that's keen –
            Still – I prefer the Damascene …

(Switching to another sword.)
This one's supple as a lash –
Valiant and full of dash!
Sparks she struck from many a hide,
For many, as pro memoria,
She whispered in the victim's ear,
Her motto as she whistled near:
(Brandishing the sword.)
"Scarce a glint as I ascend –
But when I hiss, await your end!"

(Enter PAPKIN, while DYNDALSKI, after helping the SQUIRE to buckle on the Damascene sword, exits by the door left.)

SQUIRE:	You're back!
PAPKIN:	*(Hat aslant, dress awry.)*
	And tinder-dry, God knows!
	I'll help myself, if you'll permit –
	(Pours himself a drink and downs it.)
	I let him have it on the nose –
	Enough to swell it triple size!
SQUIRE:	He's off! Another pack of lies!
PAPKIN:	That Notary's a jaunty wit –
	Infernal villain underneath!
	I often came within an ace
	Of rashly drawing sword from sheath!
	To tell the truth, I was afraid;
	Let Artemis just sniff my hand –
	And devils couldn't check that blade!
SQUIRE:	Did ever rogue tell lies so bland?
	Look, did the Notary *agree*?
PAPKIN:	I was received quite civilly,
	He game me wine – though not mature –
SQUIRE:	*(As to himself.)*
	Most likely poisoned –

81

PAPKIN:	What, the wine?
SQUIRE:	Oh, never mind –
PAPKIN:	Yes, but –
SQUIRE:	Proceed!
PAPKIN:	Poisoned, you said?
SQUIRE:	With such a swine,

Who knows what tricks he mighn't play?

PAPKIN:	I've got a pain! That's all I need!
SQUIRE:	My challenge? What did Milczek say?

Well?

(Silence.)

Deaf and dumb? Now, what's the matter?

(PAPKIN, eyes downcast and speechless, hands the SQUIRE the NOTARY's letter.)

Oh! He's written me a letter …
(Reads it.)
What's all this? What? What? What?
What?

(SQUIRE advances on PAPKIN in towering rage shouting "What" at every step, as though lost for words. PAPKIN retreats behind the table left.)

PAPKIN:	It's . . it's . . it's . . it's a fiendish plot!
SQUIRE:	The widow Anna's –
PAPKIN:	*(Dolefully.)*

– tricked us both!

SQUIRE:	The Notary's –
PAPKIN:	*(Almost in tears.)*

– secured her troth –

SQUIRE:	The Notary? That can't be right!

She means to wed –

PAPKIN:	*(In terror.)*

His son and heir!

SQUIRE:	She kept it dark! Damned fly-by-night!

82

I'll soon put paid to this affair!
O traitor sex, devoid of honour –
If I could lay my hands upon her,
I'd crush her, like this letter here!
(Crumpling the letter.)
I'd –

PAPKIN: *(Aside.)*
You'll be for it, Anna dear!

SQUIRE: Grind her piecemeal! Blast romance!
Except, there's no time to lose!
I'll lead that pair some wedding-dance –
Though not the measure they would choose!
The tune I'll play upon my fiddle
Will spin the Notary till he drops!
And, by the time the music stops,
He'll know better than to meddle …
Hi, there, servants – grooms as well –
Follow me! We'll give them hell!

(Exit SQUIRE by centre door. PAPKIN, alone, after long silence, crosses himself and feels his stomach.)

PAPKIN: It's aching … burning … I could die!
Some wine! The dregs – and poisoned, too!
You criminal! You murderer, you!
To blight so fine a rose in flower!

(DYNDALSKI enters by door left.)
Dyndalski, never known to lie –
Speak! Could this be my final hour?

DYNDALSKI: Could what?

PAPKIN: Could the Notary –
Fiend incarnate! Vicious snake!
Have poisoned Papkin? Why, oh why?

DYNDALSKI: What next?

PAPKIN: You don't believe it, then?

DYNDALSKI:	Who on earth would with to take The life of Papkin, least of men?
PAPKIN:	Such villainy you wouldn't credit?
DYNDALSKI:	No –
PAPKIN:	And yet, the Squire thought so –
DYNDALSKI:	Ah, that's different! If he said it! Nothing his honour doesn't know That's been revealed to human ken: The world is like his private den! Poison! That's a filthy trick!
PAPKIN:	Advise me! I appeal to you! What on earth am I to do?
DYNDALSKI:	*(Takes pinch of snuff.)* Perhaps we'd better call a priest! *(Leaving by centre door.)* The man's a wicked lunatic!
PAPKIN:	*(Throwing himself into a chair.)* To die! To die! Life will have ceased! *(Short silence.)* Why haven't I my wits about me? I smothered him in vile abuse – Then made him serve that poisoned juice! The speed with which he brought it out Should certainly have made me doubt: The way he tilted up the bottle, Glass after glass, as though my throttle Were a tank. Yes, I admit, Poison I swilled and relished it! Best write my will before I'm dead: *(Weeping in genuine distress.)* Then pay for my eternal bed, Meet funeral costs and burial fee – Then, farewell Papkin – R.I.P.!

(PAPKIN writes, frequently wiping tears from his eyes. Enter the SQUIRE and DYNDALSKI.)

SQUIRE: Hold hard! Stand by! There's been a change!
My first reaction was hot air - -
Revenge more subtle I'll arrange
By outmanoeuvring that pair!
To catch young Waclaw in my net,
Will be by far the safest bet!
The father doesn't worry me …
As for you –
(To PAPKIN.)
Just leave us be!

PAPKIN: *(Not looking up.)*
I'm working on my testament!

SQUIRE: Be quiet! Or I'll have you sent
Straight to the hospice for the crazed!

PAPKIN: *(Rising.)*
You will?
(Aside.)
That's one bequest erased!
(PAPKIN moves to a table, left of stage.)

SQUIRE: *(To DYNDALSKI.)*
You sit down and ink your quill;
I've a letter to dictate …

DYNDALSKI: I'm not the world's best writer … still –

SQUIRE: A girlish hand I want to see –
Convent taught – the perfect bait
To captivate a flirt!

DYNDALSKI: *(Sits down facing the Squire, profile to audience and puts on his spectacles.)*
Praise be!

SQUIRE: Now listen, you are going to write
As from Clara to young Waclaw –

DYNDALSKI: Oh no!

SQUIRE:	What?
DYNDALSKI:	*(Rising.)*

Squire – if I might –
She'd be disgraced by such an act!

SQUIRE:	Who's asking you, sir, what you think?

Sit down and dip your quill in ink?

(DYNDALSKI sits with outstretched legs on the edge of the chair and dips his quill in the ink-well. Throughout this scene, PAPKIN is also writing. He gets up every so often to ink his quill at the table where the SQUIRE is sitting, then returns to his seat, weeping discretely.)

SQUIRE:	*(After a pause for reflection.)*

We must take care, for it's a fact
That good deception is an art!
Love-lorn chit-chat will attract –
Idle twitter warms the heart!
(Ponders.)
How do you think I ought to start?

DYNDALSKI:	*(Rising.)*

Devotedly, love of my life!

SQUIRE:	That's to a husband from his wife!

Half those words, or less, will do – -
She can't decide; she's in a stew!
"I'd like to, but I just don't dare - -"
Come on . . you know . . it's quite an art –
Albeit late for you to start!
Just write –
(Humming to himself.)
Now, here we go –
(Hums as he dictates.)
Write "Please"
(Looking across at the paper.)
What's that?

DYNDALSKI: *(Rising, as always when he addresses the SQUIRE.)*
Why, it's a "P" –

SQUIRE: Indeed?

DYNDALSKI: Yes, its capital "P", what else?

SQUIRE: *(Peering across the table.)*
I see the stroke, but where's the paunch?

DYNDALSKI: Above the line, the paunch sticks out –

SQUIRE: *(Adjusting spectacles.)*
God's teeth!
(Picks up sheet of paper.)
A "P", you say? I doubt –
(PAPKIN leans across in front of the SQUIRE, wanting to ink his quill. SQUIRE pushes him aside.)
Get back!
(PAPKIN, repulsed, moves away. SQUIRE follows him with his eyes. PAPKIN treads on DYNDALSKI's foot in passing.)

DYNDALSKI: Ouch!

SQUIRE: *(Peering at letter.)*
Capital "P", you say?
Might make it out in time, perhaps!
Right, carry on!   No more mishaps!
(SQUIRE dictates.)
"Please …" Why, yes, that's it, I feel –
Now, yes – that's it – hum – "my appeal …"
That's it, good, good – yes, "should be taken
As sign of confidence – unshaken" –
That's it, good! – "in yourself alone,
One who, albeit little known –
One who, albeit little known …"
(Pointing at letter again.)
What's that?

DYNDALSKI:	*(Rising to his feet.)* A blot, a splash of ink – But I can write it in, I think –
SQUIRE:	Any more drops and dribbles, fool, And I will box your ears so red, You'll swear you're back at infant-school! Now, read it – *(DYNDALSKI wipes perspiration from face and neck.)* If it can be read!
DYNDALSKI:	"Please why yes that's it I feel, Now yes hum that's it my appeal – That's it good hum, yes, should be taken – Good, yes, that is, should be taken –"
SQUIRE:	*(Snatches paper and tears it into pieces.)* Confound you! "Hum" you even wrote! You stupid, brainless nanny-goat!
DYNDALSKI:	But Squire, your very words, I swear!
SQUIRE:	Shut up! Now copy it with care, Leave out "good", "hum" and the rest –
DYNDALSKI:	*(Trying to piece together the torn scraps.)* Tricky – but I'll do my best!
SQUIRE:	Write it out again, I say! You pudding-headed imbecile! Sit down! Sit down!
DYNDALSKI:	Yes, if I may –
SQUIRE:	Now, once again *(Dictating.)* "Please, my appeal –" Hum – – *(Clapping hand to mouth.)*
DYNDALSKI:	*(Reading over what he has written.)* My appeal hum –

SQUIRE:	*(Starting up in a rage.)*
	What's that "hum" supposed to be?
	This dunce will never write a letter!
	I'll have to do it differently –
	Who knows? It might be even better
	To send by word of mouth, instead
	Of trusting such a dunderhead!
	You'd better go! But, no – just wait!
	Nobody knows the Notary's son –
	Nobody on my estate – -
PAPKIN:	*(Calmly, weak voice.)*
	He's been seen by everyone!
	Came here today – -
SQUIRE:	What? That young pup?
	That so-called agent is his son?
PAPKIN:	None other –
SQUIRE:	Monstrous! I give up!
	You let that fox my home invade?
	Without a word? I've been betrayed!
PAPKIN:	*(Indifferently.)*
	He bought my silence with his gold …
SQUIRE:	*(Head in hands.)*
	You scoundrel! Villain! I've been sold!
PAPKIN:	With one foot firmly in the grave,
	It makes me laugh to hear you rave!
	(Flings purse on the floor.)
	Can lucre help in my position?
SQUIRE:	Silence!
PAPKIN:	Worthless coin! I mock it!
	What good is gold in my condition?
	(DYNDALSKI moves to pick up purse but PAPKIN quickly forestalls him.)
	Except for putting in the pocket!

SQUIRE:	*(To PAPKIN.)*
	Easy! Far too much excitement;
	No time now for your indictment –
	But, as a noble worth my salt,
	I'll make you pay for that default!
	(Turning to DYNDALSKI.)
	Go at once and fine old Rosie –
	Send her round to Milczek's home!
	She's to tell the Notary's son –
	Waclaw – yes, she'll know the one,
	That young Miss Clara bids him come!
	Not a word must he betray –
	But kindly hasten to appear.
	Above all, say he need not fear
	Because the Squire has gone away!
	Is that understood?
DYNDALSKI:	Completely!
SQUIRE:	Meanwhile, you arrange discreetly
	For an ambush on his way –
	In the bushes by the wall.
	Once he steps across the border,
	Seize the puppy – that's an order!
	Bind him if you must. That's all!
DYNDALSKI:	It's dishonourable, Squire,
	To treat him as a common thief!
SQUIRE:	Addlepate beyond belief!
	Go and do as I require!
	(SQUIRE, on point of leaving, is intercepted by PAPKIN.)
PAPKIN:	Squire!
SQUIRE:	What?
PAPKIN:	*(Holding out his will.)*
	Witness Papkin's will!
SQUIRE:	Be hanged to you!

(Exit SQUIRE and DYNDALSKI by centre door.)

PAPKIN:
                                  "Be hanged to you!"
No gratitude … no credit due!
Each for himself! The only rule –
Your fellow-man is just your tool!
While all goes well, the world is yours,
But down and out – you're on all fours!
(Enter CLARA through door right.)
O Goddess of my thoughts, divine!
Compassion you alone dispense!
Poison has sheared life's filaments
But still my heart, as in a shrine,
Preserves my love for you intact!

CLARA: What's wrong?

PAPKIN:
                              I'm good as dead, in fact!
I meant to fetch your crocodile,
And would have sought your hand to gain,
But life, which lasts so short a while,
Today will end this warrior's pain!

CLARA: *(Aside.)*
His mind's completely gone, I fear!

PAPKIN: My testament to you I leave:
Deign, like a mother, to give ear –
And, later, by my tomb to grieve …
(PAPKIN reads out his will, frequently wiping a tear from his eye.)
I, Joseph Papkin, son of my father John,
being of sound mind and body, though not
knowing when I shall die – obviously –
because I have been poisoned by the Notary
Milczek with a glass of wine –
a glass of wine –
do hereby make this will or final disposition

of my goods and chattels.   Of my goods I cannot
dispose, because I have none – so cannot –
as for my chattels, I distribute them thus:
to her whom I have always loved, honoured,
revered and deified – to Clara – I bequeath my
English guitar and collection of rare butterflies,
being now in pawn. My trusty Artemis –
I meant the Squire to have my sword,
But that bequest has now been scored!
– Artemis, my sword, I leave to the bravest
warrior in all Europe, provided he will erect a
monument on my grave. With my remaining
chattels,
I wish to be interred.
(Wipes a tear.)
As Executor and Executrix respectively of this
will, I name His Honour the Squire, and Clara
his niece, begging them to refrain from meeting
any debts of mine which may present themselves
from whatever quarter, in order thereby to
bequeath a permanent memento to my brothers of
various stations and denominations ... .
Joseph Papkin.
Papkin, further not described -
For ranks and titles, there's no space –
Take this will! May what's inscribed
Your memory for ever grace!

(Enter WACLAW through door left.)

WACLAW:	Dear Clara, I don't understand –
	We're harassed by too cruel a fate!
	The hopes we cherished, all we planned,
	Now threaten to disintegrate!
CLARA:	*(With a side glance at PAPKIN.)*
	Watch what you say!

92

WACLAW:	Oh, he's been paid!
	The widow's now at our address.
	The plan my heartless father's made
	Is that I marry her perforce!
CLARA:	God help us!
WACLAW:	And that creature – coarse –
	Devoid of shame and pitiless –
	Not caring where my love inclines,
	Has lent herself to his designs.
CLARA:	Waclaw, I'm not competent
	To offer counsel in your plight.
	Your presence here fills me with fright!
	You just don't know my uncle's rage –
	His fury cannot be contained!
WACLAW:	Have no worry on that score:
	I'm Milczek's agent – nothing more!
PAPKIN:	*(Indifferently.)*
	That fiction cannot be maintained …
WACLAW:	Then you've betrayed –
PAPKIN:	I told the truth –
WACLAW:	You scoundrel!
CLARA:	*(Restraining him.)*
	No, please! Waclaw, dear!
	I beg you – don't increase my fear!
WACLAW:	At least, let me give him his due –
CLARA:	You'll kill your Clara if you do!
PAPKIN:	To someone lying at death's door,
	Threats don't matter any more …
WACLAW:	What's he say?
CLARA:	A pointless row!
	Escape quick! Every second counts!
PAPKIN:	She's right! Take my advice: go now!
	The Squire intends, by all accounts,

	To lure you here, have you waylaid:
	He's posted men in ambuscade
	To seize you and, if need be, bind you!
CLARA:	Still unconvinced! Don't let them find you!
WACLAW:	What shall we do?
CLARA:	*(Fearfully.)*
	I'll write, don't worry.
WACLAW:	This evening!
CLARA:	I hear voices – hurry!
WACLAW:	But as I said –
CLARA:	*(Beseeching.)* Please, wait till then!
WACLAW:	All right – but I'll be back again!

(As WACLAW moves towards door left, enter the SQUIRE, DYNDALSKI and SERVANTS from different doors.)

SQUIRE:	*(Barring way to door left.)*
	How now? I've caught you, honey-bear!
	The keeper has been on your track!
WACLAW:	What if he has? Should I despair?
	I see that adversaries don't lack –
	But don't imagine I'm afraid!
	(To SQUIRE.)
	If you're a brigand, I'm waylaid –
	But if you are a man of merit,
	Why not, with sword, conclusions try?
	The good Lord willing, I'll not die!
SQUIRE:	I like a man who shows some spirit!
	But no such duel is in question …
	Instead, pay heed to my suggestion …
	The Notary stole my bride-to-be,
	To marry you instead of me.
	He thought he'd score and leave me flat:
	But I know tricks worth two of that!

94

Either I'll lock you in the keep,
Where none would ever guess you sleep –
Or else, to Clara you'll be wed.
Should she refuse to tie the know,
She's got a cousin, gently bred:
You'll marry her instead! Why not?
For you, a wife of nymph-like charm;
The widow keeps a lonely bed;
The Notary suffers grievous harm –
And my *revenge* will be complete:
The case disposed of – short and sweet!

(Silence.)

WACLAW: But –

SQUIRE: No buts! Don't hesitate!

WACLAW: Now?

SQUIRE: If not, you'll be too late!

WACLAW: *(To CLARA.)*
Dare we believe him?

CLARA: Seems we must!
(To the SQUIRE.)
This day we'll wed?

SQUIRE: Now!

(CLARA looks at WACLAW, awaiting answer.)

WACLAW: Then, let's trust!

SQUIRE: Give the girl your hand, don't falter!
She's not disinclined, I see –
The priest's already at the altar!
Lead on!
(Aside.)
Hang the Notary!
(They pass into the chapel.)

PAPKIN: O tigress Fortune, heartlss Fate!
Poison, weddings, drama such –

95

I'm overcome!   It's all too much!
(PAPKIN follows them into chapel.)

DYNDALSKI: *(Picking up scraps of letter.)*

Bees in the bonnet, once installed,
Are devilishly heard to put to flight!
I never thought that I'd be called –
Long as I've lived in God's good sight –
To write dictation for the Squire!
Presumption such, no doubt, was sin –
Yet, might I all the same, inquire
Why – at my age – should I begin
To learn my ABC, and why
Did he make such a point of "P" –
That letter in particular?
Wrong size? Not perpendicular?
A heavy cross – still, I will try!

(Sits down and starts piecing the scraps together. Enter the NOTARY, peering about him. He approaches DYNDALSKI, who hasn't seen him, laying his hand on his arm.)

NOTARY: Good evening! Somebody's about!
I thought a plague had wiped them out!
No living soul and none to say
The Squire is here or gone away!

DYNDALSKI: He's here.   Your servant, sir!

NOTARY: It's strange!
His Honour challenged me to fight.
Though not a pastime I'd arrange,
I said "let heaven's will be done,
Acclaimed by all opposed by none!"
So out I went and waited there
With nought to do but take the air:
Perhaps too rashly he assumed
That his opponent would retire.

96

If so, quite wrongly he presumed;
The one not present was the Squire!

DYNDALSKI: Illustrious sir, take my advice –
Don't give the Squire a chance to slice:
He'll snip your every loop and button –
Carve you – like a leg of mutton!

VOICES: (*From the chapel.*)
Long live, long live the happy pair!

NOTARY: Whose wedding's going on in there?

DYNDALSKI: Your son's –

NOTARY: *(As though scalded.)*
It isn't possible!

SQUIRE: *(Offstage.)*
Dyndalski, what are you waiting for?
Saddle my charger! I must go!
(Appearing.)
Damn and blast, it's long past four!

(SQUIRE advances to front of stage, catches sight of the NOTARY and stands as if petrified. NOTARY bows low. They glare at one another for a few moments in silence. SQUIRE reaches for his sword, as does the NOTARY. Pause for reflection. SQUIRE appears to be struggling to control himself. DYNDALSKI runs towards the chapel.)
Lead me not into temptation!
Great Lord of my fathers, stay my arm!
Once within my habitation,
No hair of his shall suffer harm!

(He unbuckles his belt and throws his sword on the table. NOTARY hangs his hat on his own sword-hilt.)
What do you want?

NOTARY: I want my boy!

SQUIRE: Nothing could give me greater joy!
You'll be content, I'll stake my life –

	But, with her? Or without his wife?
NOTARY:	*(Restraining himself.)*
	This is too much!
SQUIRE:	How so? It's clear –

You stole my widow, as we saw –
To make her your daughter-in-law.
I trapped your son and thought it best
To celebrate his wedding here;
You've been repaid with interest!

(SQUIRE and NOTARY are now joined by CLARA, WACLAW, PAPKIN, DYNDALSKI, staff and women who emerge from the chapel with bouquets of flowers.)

WACLAW:	Father!
CLARA:	Uncle! Pray resolve
	This confusion so distressing!
WACLAW:	*(He Kneels.)*
	Father, pardon! Hear my plea –
	Grant our love paternal blessing!
NOTARY:	Rise, my son, and come with me!

(Enter the WIDOW.)

WIDOW:	Must I credit what would seem . . ?
	Waclaw … Clara … ?
PAPKIN:	*(Aside.)*
	It's a dream!
WIDOW:	So be it … What is done is done!

Let me explain to everyone:
To wed I was in such a hurry,
Driven by fear of want and worry.
Those farms and forests left to me
Were only mine in trust, you see,
To hold till Clara's wedding-day …
They're hers – to cherish as she may!

98

NOTARY: *(Aside.)*

Two good estates – a tasty morsel –
And for the Squire, a sharp reversal!

SQUIRE: *(Aside.)*

For me, as uncle, profit lacks –
I've swapped a cudgel for my axe!

WIDOW: But I'm at least, entitled to
(Pointing at NOTARY.)
The hundred thousand, which he owes!

CLARA: Not he, but I will pay what's due!
(WIDOW moves to right of stage. CLARA to NOTARY.)
Pray, don't continue to oppose,
Let anger's shreds be swept away
And bless your children's wedding day!
(She kneels down with WACLAW to whom she gives her right hand.)

NOTARY: Let Heaven's will on earth be done,
Acclaimed by all, opposed by none!
(NOTARY blesses them and helps them up.)

PAPKIN: *(To WACLAW.)*

But can I on your word rely?
You swear I'm not about to die?
(After affirmative nod, PAPKIN turns to SQUIRE.)
Why the, Squire – take my challenge up!
Let servants bring the loving-cup!
Let fanfares sound and trumpets blare –
And let's all toast the happy pair!

(PAPKIN moves to left of stage and tears up his will.)

SQUIRE: In heart and deed, let's make of this
A wedding-day of matchless bliss!
(Offering his hand to the NOTARY.)
Between us, honoured sir, be peace!
(NOTARY accepts his hand, bows low.)

ALL: Peace and concord!

WACLAW: *(Stepping into centre, while CLARA on his right*
                     gives her hand to the SQUIRE and WACLAW
                     takes the hand of his father on the left. They all
                     move forward.)
                                    Troubles at an end –
                     Now, may the Lord His hand to us extend!

                     THE END

REVENGE
[ŚLUBY PANIÉNSKIE]

This translation of *Virgins' Vows* was presented by the BBC
World Service in August 1992. The cast was as follows:

PANI DOBRUSKA	Frances Jeater
ANIELA	Julia Ford
CLARA	Zelah Clarke
RADOST	Edward de Souza
GUSTAVE	Robert Glenister
ALBIN	Adam Godley
JAN	Timothy Bateson
DIRECTOR	Gordon House

The play is set in the Polish countryside – mainly at the
home of Madame Dobruska, early in the nineteenth
century.

ACT ONE

SCENE ONE

Large room in PANI DOBRUSKA's house. Two doors at rear and a third door, right of stage, leading to PANI DOBRUSKA's own apartments. Fourth door, left of stage, leads to GUSTAVE's room. A window.

JAN:	*(Alone, walking with cape thrown over his shoulders. Looks back through window; yawns as he speaks.)*
	Be back by three, he says. Don't go to bed!
	I like that! Three! Broad daylight! I'm half-dead:
	And my young master whiles the night away,
	Gaming or tippling – or – I'd best not say!
RADOST:	Gustave sleeping?
JAN:	Sound as in the grave . . .
RADOST:	The rascal likes his rest!
JAN:	*(Barring the way to GUSTAVE's room.)* Sir, let him be!
RADOST:	But why?
JAN:	He's fast asleep . . .
RADOST:	He won't mind me.
JAN:	*(Stepping in front of him.)*
	He gets so angry . . .
RADOST:	Nonsense, let him rave!
JAN:	He just dropped off – not half an hour ago!
RADOST:	What kept him up?
JAN:	He couldn't sleep –
RADOST:	How so?
JAN:	Came over faint –
RADOST:	Faint?
JAN:	Yes . . . a sudden swoon . . .

RADOST: What's wrong with him?

JAN: Some sort of giddy spell –

RADOST: Hmmm –

JAN: Fear of water.....

RADOST: Hmmmm –

JAN: A thirst for wine!

RADOST: Come, come! Why, yesterday he seemed quite well!

JAN: *(With a shrug.)*
But faintness strikes, just when you're feeling fine!

RADOST: *(Aside.)*
These fears and cravings? Hmmm? A giddy spell?

JAN: He'll sleep his fill, get up this afternoon.

RADOST: I meant to go home first – come back – then call;
The way things are, though, that won't do at all!

JAN: Oh yes, do go, sir! By the time you're back –

RADOST: He's sleeping soundly?

JAN: *(Barring his way.)* Quietly, sir – I pray you!
The slightest noise –

RADOST: I'll open it a crack.

JAN: The hinges squeak –

RADOST: I must be satisfied –

JAN: *(Stepping aside.)*
In that case, sir, I'd better not delay you . . .
No point your looking, though, he's not inside.

RADOST: Not there?

JAN: No, sir.

RADOST: Where? When?

JAN: Alas, alack!

RADOST: How... ? What?

JAN: He left –

RADOST: Where for?

JAN: Lublin, he said –

RADOST: Lu-lu –

JAN: *(Bows as he completes the word.)*
            – blin.

RADOST: When?

JAN: Yesterday –

RADOST: But why?

JAN: Don't know –

RADOST: You see? He's going off his head!
            Sneaks out at night and leaves you standing by.
            What is all this? You and your fainting-fits!
            This talk of hydrophobia and thirst for wine?

JAN: I'm keeping watch, sir, by the window. Its
            My job to open up at the first sign –

RADOST: What of?

JAN: That master's waiting, pray!
            As he goes out – so he comes in again.

RADOST: *(Wringing hands.)*
            What? Clambers through the window in broad day?
            That proves it! No mistake! The lad's insane!
            (Sarcastic.)
            The day he weds, I take it, he'll be there?

JAN: To be back here by three was what he planned.

RADOST: It's all too much, far more than I can bear!
            I've simply got to take that boy in hand …

            Tapping is heard at the window.

JAN: That 's him, sir, now – so you just have your say.

            *Opens the window to let in GUSTAVE, in riding-costume.
            RADOST stands well back as GUSTAVE creeps in.*

GUSTAVE: Appalling weather! Devil of a day!

JAN: You're right, sir. There'll be hell to pay, I think!

GUSTAVE:	All still abed?
JAN:	That, sir, would be some sleep!
GUSTAVE:	I'm slightly late –
JAN:	Slightly's a trifle steep!
GUSTAVE:	You must have slept your fill?
JAN:	Not slept a wink!
GUSTAVE:	*(Gives JAN his riding-crop, cap, gloves. Mopping his face.)*

GUSTAVE:
What filthy weather! Sure as I was born,
I've never heard my teeth make such a din!
Wind, rain and cold! 'Twould keep a mongrel in –

RADOST: But, Nephew, you've been out in it till morn!

GUSTAVE: Uncle!

Kisses his hand.

Good-day to you!

RADOST: *(Coldly.)*
I greet the stray!

GUSTAVE: Up early?

RADOST: Late to bed?

GUSTAVE: Not yet.

RADOST: Mid-day!

GUSTAVE: Come, barely dawn!

RADOST: Dawn in your eyes …

GUSTAVE:
Be that as it may! Here's to the new day's rise!
So long as my dear Uncle loves me ever,
I shall be hale and hearty – perish never!
What's this I see? A frown! The devil take it!
(Peering into his eyes.)
A twinkle in the eye? Much less severe;
And now the forehead … smooth as you can make it?
That's how I like to see you …
(Embracing him.)
Uncle, dear!

RADOST:	*(Plaintive, admonishing.)*
	Do you, or don't you, Gustave – want a wife?
GUSTAVE:	I do!
RADOST:	Quite sure?
GUSTAVE:	The yearning fills my life!
RADOST:	But is this any way to satisfy it?
GUSTAVE:	I've really no idea; I'll not deny it.
RADOST:	Nocturnal forays? Sneaking in and out?
GUSTAVE:	What of it?
RADOST:	Spare her feelings!
GUSTAVE:	What about?

I fail to see her concern
When, how or where I sleep – go or return,
The better for her the longer I am awake –
My every conscious thought here to partake.
All day and night, I yearn – each waking hour!
Were I to sleep, would that be in my power?

RADOST: *(Pleading.)*

Gustave, dear boy, this flippancy reject!
Once in your life, at least, take pause – reflect!
These past few days, you've been this family's guest,
Yet not an hour's gone by but you've professed
Heart-rending disregard for good behaviour –
Pani Dobruska's care has been your saviour.
Unlike so many mothers, nose-in-the-air,
While bending heaven's ear in secret prayer
For sons-in-law, she's voiced faith in you –
Thanks to your parents' friendship and mine, too.
But what's the use? Her trouble's been in vain:
The dandy treats the peasants with disdain!
He's bored and rudely makes his hosts aware
They're stealing precious time he ill can spare.
Sparrows nest in empty roofs, tis said –
But even sparrows wouldn't choose your head!

GUSTAVE: *(Sincerely.)*
             True, Uncle! I have earned your stern displeasure!
             You've watched me with a father's loving eyes –
             (Embracing him.)
             And every warning I sincerely prize:
             Thank you, dear Uncle, your advice I treasure!

RADOST: *(Deeply moved, embraces him.)*
             Gustave, my own dear, honourable boy!

GUSTAVE: My uncle, friend and father! You've succeeded!
             The change in me you will observe with joy.
             Reason to mend my ways was all I needed . .
             Now, guess the party I was at last night!

RADOST: Lord, he's incorrigible! Change, is right!
             For pity's sake! What way to woo is that?
             Creep out the window like a guilty cat
             And God knows what you do all night – and where!

GUSTAVE: A man must have some fun … that's only fair

RADOST: Fun!

GUSTAVE: Fact is, in this fine residence
             Where I've been treated … yes, too graciously –
             And where I neither give nor take offence –
             A little fun and games I've yet to see!

RADOST: Are parties all you think of? Din and whirl?

GUSTAVE: I'm bored, that's all!

RADOST: Bored? By a pretty girl?

GUSTAVE: I won't be bored, once I can love her, true …

RADOST: And when will that be?

GUSTAVE: Once I'm married to her.

RADOST: More like it, when the girl has jilted you!

GUSTAVE: Not likely!

RADOST: Why so sure you needn't woo her?
             Is it ordained, somewhere in heaven above,
             That Aniela must give you her love?

GUSTAVE: She'll marry me, all right –

RADOST: Your faith amazes;
             But I can't bear to hear you sing your praises!

GUSTAVE: You'd hardly call me boastful if I state –
             Having most carefully assessed the case –
             That when two families mean to integrate,
             One may assume a wedding will take place.

RADOST: Provided Aniela feels well-matched …

GUSTAVE: She favours me, on that you may depend.
             All will be well, I wager, in the end!

RADOST: Chickens are best not counted till they're hatched.

GUSTAVE: Leave it to me! But – no more proverbs, please.
             You've still not guessed, though, where I took my ease.

RADOST: Indeed … Where were you?

GUSTAVE: Where I stayed so long?

RADOST: Out with it, man! The devil loose your tongue!

GUSTAVE: A costume ball … All dancers in disguise …

RADOST: But where?

GUSTAVE: "The Golden Parrot Inn", it's called.

RADOST: An inn?

GUSTAVE: I was disguised …

RADOST: I'm still appalled!

GUSTAVE: What harm? One's young. What's there to criticise?

RADOST: *(Ironic.)* I'm meant to praise it, am I?

GUSTAVE: Why not, pray?

RADOST: What an academy!

GUSTAVE: The best, I'd say!
             Among small-fry, puffed up by artifice,
             Where gingerly each treads the slippery ice –
             As though on stilts and with his visor down –
             No man's true worth can ever be divined!
             But where, on false display, none sets a price,
             Nor bird in borrowed plumage craves renown –

And man is governed more by heart than mind –
That's where one draws from nature, fair and square!

RADOST: So, that's your line! Another La Bruyère!
(Plaintively.)
You welcomed my advice, you called me kind …

GUSTAVE: *(Not listening.)*
I've had a brainwave, touching this affair!

RADOST: What?

GUSTAVE: Let us –

RADOST: You and I?

GUSTAVE: An evening out!

RADOST: You're mad!

GUSTAVE: Home early …

RADOST: *(Ironic.)*   Secretly, no doubt …

GUSTAVE: Will you?

RADOST: Not likely!

GUSTAVE: Then I'll go alone!

RADOST: You welcomed my advice; said you'd atone …

GUSTAVE: *(Doleful.)*
Dear Uncle, I'll be married all too soon …

RADOST: *(To himself, astonished.)*
That's why he's acting like a chuckle-head!

GUSTAVE: *(Sadly, pleading voice.)*
Only once more –

RADOST: Can't make him change his tune!
No use …

GUSTAVE: I'll ride the chestnut mare tonight.

RADOST: *(Alarmed.)* The chestnut?

GUSTAVE: I'll be back before it's light …

RADOST: No, not the chestnut! Take my fly instead …

(Aside.)
He'll break his neck, the fool, and no mistake!

GUSTAVE: So be it …

RADOST: Take my fur-lined mantle, pray!

GUSTAVE: Thanks …

RADOST: You'll catch your death, for heaven's sake!
That coat you're wearing's like a summer vest.

GUSTAVE: It shall be as you wish … Uncle knows best!
You give superb advice, I always say …

RADOST: He'll claim it's on my advice, the crafty devil,
As he creeps out the window to his revel!

GUSTAVE: Would you suggest I knock at the front door
On my return?

RADOST: You're mad! I'll say no more!
Sleep is what I advise …

GUSTAVE: Sleep?

RADOST: You look rotten!

GUSTAVE: Pale? What of that? No harm, I'm sure:
A loss of colour proves love's pangs endure!
Unlike mere words, pallor precludes deceit …
Uncle, I'm sure you have not forgotten
The morning after you stood us all a treat!

RADOST: My treat?

GUSTAVE: In a sense, I s'pose you're right:
I was the host myself – and what a night!
But later, Uncle, it was you who paid …

RADOST: Alas!

GUSTAVE: As for my face – a woeful shade …
"The boy's in love! There's not the slightest doubt
So pale and weak, he'll likely not last out!"
True, is it not? Was that not what they said?
And if I hadn't been …

RADOST:	Get off to bed!
	No end to it! He tells me now … Quite mad!
	Look, sleep is what you need and I'd be glad
	If you'd take my advice, Gustave, dear Gus:
	Pay court to Aniela! Try to please her …

GUSTAVE: Yes, Uncle –

RADOST: And respect Mama – don't tease her!

GUSTAVE: No, Uncle –

RADOST: And mark well, in this connection –
If you set any story by my affection –
Just think before you speak, restrain your chatter;
Don't spray words out as though they didn't matter!
You talk sheer rubbish, babble without thinking!
Away with you and get some sleep – you're blinking!

GUSTAVE: I'll go and change –
(Kisses his hand.)

RADOST: *(Kissing GUSTAVE.)* Bear what I say in mind!

GUSTAVE: The change in me, you'll be amazed to find!
(Exit GUSTAVE by side door left.)

RADOST: *(Watching him go, with serious expression.)*
Change! Every day and hour – the same old play!
Amazed I'd be! That's true …
(With sudden show of emotion.) The darling boy!
(Enter ALBIN.)
Albin! How come, so early in the day?
Your woeful sighing fills me with dismay.

ALBIN: *(Handkerchief in hand, tragic voice.)*
Should I not sigh, all but in sorrow drowned –
Awake all night, weeping the clock around?

RADOST: I would advise you to relax, my boy!
Don't copy Gustave, but mix love with joy!
These doleful plaints and maundering laments
Will never win a young girl's confidence –
Least of all, Clara's! She's a merry spark;

	Sighs when she yawns – but cheerful as a lark!

Sighs when she yawns – but cheerful as a lark!
Hardly a moment still – and silent rarely –
A joyous disposition, if contrary.
You, sir, are misery incarnate! That she fears!

ALBIN: How can one be in love and not in tears?
It's two years now since Clara's charm, her treasure,
Kindled in me a passion past all measure.
No day but I, with soulful glance implore:
If I refrained from sighs – I'd breathe no more!
Her steps I've traced with tears, her path bestrewn:
My tears would melt a stone – but she's immune!

RADOST: You'd weep a hundred years – she wouldn't care!
(ALBIN groans deeply.)
You've nothing else in mind?

ALBIN: Death from despair!

RADOST: What if she loved you?

ALBIN: I would die for joy!

RADOST: The bells would toll in either case, my boy!

ALBIN: I weep; you mock –

RADOST: Then why not laugh with me?

ALBIN: Listen to what I say and you'll soon see …
I hoped devotion would extinguish hate,
Breed milder feelings, harmony create:
But men she loathes as such, without concession.
She revels in it, proud of her obsession!
I've been a fool! In vain do I aspire:
Her heart grows colder, while my own's on fire!

RADOST: Farewell!

ALBIN: You're going?

RADOST: Must go home. I'm late!

ALBIN: You're quite unmoved! You leave me to my fate?

RADOST: I have to go. I've lingered far too long –
(Consulting watch.)

	I should be there, unless I've got it wrong –
	That comes of humouring an addlepate
	Whose motto is to let all problems wait.
ALBIN:	*(Clutching his hand.)*
	Please! I've a dreadful secret to convey –
RADOST:	Good Lord, what now?
ALBIN:	I'll tell you, if you'll stay …
RADOST:	You frighten me!
ALBIN:	Discretion guaranteed?
RADOST:	Speak!
ALBIN:	Clara and Aniela have agreed …
	Hear me and weep – never to wed!
RADOST:	*(Surprised, trying not to laugh.)*
	No! True?

ALBIN nods; RADOST laughs.

ALBIN:	Funny?
RADOST:	I cannot credit that! Can you?
ALBIN:	I swear …
RADOST:	How do you know?
ALBIN:	I do …
RADOST:	If so,
	(To himself.)
	It might spur Gustave to a livelier show –
	If he believed it!
	(To ALBIN.) Well, I'm glad to hear it!
ALBIN:	Glad? When I'm at death's door – or very near it!
RADOST:	You're not! We'll both survive!
ALBIN:	You're poking fun!
RADOST:	Weep less, and fate will smile on you, my son!

Exit RADOST by left-hand door.

| ALBIN: | O Love! O Love! The cause of all my woe! |
| | I blame you not, for sweet the tears that flow! |

But when will she repay me equally?
Clara! Clara! Clara! Will you weep with me?

Enter ANIELA and CLARA, on the last line, through centre door. CLARA moves quietly into position beside ALBIN.

CLARA: Summoned not just once, but thrice –
So attractively withal –
By your triply-voiced command!
Deathless sprites to such a call,
Like well-bred children, in a trice
Would swift abandon dark designs,
And race to hear their lord's demand!
With equal promptness I've replied
And here stand waiting at your side!

ALBIN: *(Kissing her hand.)*
Aaaah!

CLARA: That's all?

ALBIN: A boon to one who pines!
(CLARA laughs. Short pause.)
You mock my love!

CLARA: Why, nothing of the kind!

ALBIN: Hard-hearted as a –

CLARA: – tigress springs to mind.

ALBIN: No man could melt your heart –

CLARA: Not *any* man, that's true!

ALBIN: I'm so in love …

CLARA: I'm not …

ALBIN: I weep for you!

CLARA: I laugh …

ALBIN: You'll recognise my worth too late!

CLARA: Cruel, heartless? What a shame! Let's leave him!
(To ANIELA.)
Quick, let's escape, for love lies here in wait!
Come on, Aniela – quickly! Don't believe him!

(Starts to sing.)
"Wherever love puts forth its snare,
Children, trifle not! Beware!
Love's no joke, for you must know –
Once you're caught, love won't let go!"
That's what we learned at Granny's knee;
Let's escape, while fancy-free!

ALBIN:
Stay, cruel one! I'll liberate your eyes
From this sad object which you so despise.
My torment pleases you? Rejoice at will!
Your every blow struck home … Each rankles still!
One consolation's mine, from guilt exempt:
Nothing I've done deserves such harsh contempt!

ANIELA:
Oh, Albin, you take everything to heart!
We meant it all in jest … Don't run away!

CLARA:
I wasn't joking, Cousin, for my part!

ALBIN:
I took your words as Gospel from the start!

CLARA:
Praised be he who's flexible, I say!

ALBIN:
But pity one by Clara's heart-strings tied –
For even *hope* of pity he's denied!

Exit ALBIN by side door right.

ANIELA:
To tease and torture him just isn't right.

CLARA:
Am I to marry him?

ANIELA:
No, sooner fly!
Let some compassion, though, assuage his plight…
You might at least explain the reason *why*!

CLARA:
No! Let the idiot love, weep, groan and – perish!

ANIELA:
Ah, Clara, no! You can't be that severe!

CLARA:
Fie on his love so-called! Freedom I cherish!

ANIELA:
But find a gentler way to make it clear –
A sign will do … It needn't all be said.

CLARA:
What? Am I then to face him, curtsey thrice?
Twisting my apron blushing lobster-red

And, stammering in an effort to be nice,
Expect him meekly to accept the fact
That I reject him, as I do all creatures male?

ANIELA: Why no, indeed? Far better show some tact,
Than tell the wretched man, to no avail,
That neither he, not yet the way he woos you,
Can please you in the slightest, or amuse you!

CLARA: Tact wouldn't work! He'd take it in his stride:
Man's heart is made of sterner stuff by far!
Each wound is swiftly hidden by a scar –
A scar which then becomes his badge of pride!
Male vanity is proof against all blows:
The more you punish it, the more it grows!
Scold them, despise them, hate them – all no use!
Men thrive on anger, loathing and abuse …
Until some poor unfortunate (not us),
Patience exhausted, worn out by the fuss,
So battle-weary that her wits elude her,
Succumbs to love for *peace* from the intruder!

ANIELA: I know all that! No word would I gainsay!
Men, too, I know – that breed of crocodile!
How cunningly they lurk in search of prey,
Betraying whomsoever they beguile!
But if *they're* wicked, must *we* follow suit?

CLARA: Women's virtue isn't in dispute.
Women *were* good but what did they achieve?
Men had their fun; women were left to grieve!
That book … remember?

ANIELA: Yes, and no mistake!
"Clorinda's Husband, or the Faithless Rake".

CLARA: *(Mounting vehemence.)*
Would you forgo revenge because one man
Grieves, having stalked in vain and lost his prize?
Determined not to wed, should we our plan,

117

By indiscreet rejection, publicise –
Destroying hope for one and all thereby,
Sparing the self-esteem of would-be swains?
Certainly not! We'll none of that, say I!
You who do boast your victory in love's campaigns –
Down on your knees, men! Bend your haughty necks!
Suffer, each one, our scorn for all your sex!

ANIELA: *(Excitedly.)*
Let them all pine!

CLARA: And love *me*, if they must!

ANIELA: Why *you*?

CLARA: Because in vain they'll lust!

ANIELA: *My* heart's set hard as yours against deception!

CLARA: Aniela, let's join hands, our vows repeat:
Victory to women and to men – defeat!

TOGETHER: *(In chorus, holding hands.)*
I swear by womanly strength of heart and head
To hate the tribe of men and never wed!

ANIELA: Hate … yes, of course … but Uncle's an exception –

CLARA: So's Daddy –

ANIELA: And my cousins – only fair!

CLARA: There's Jan –

ANIELA: - and Karol –

CLARA: – Jozef –

ANIELA: Stashek, too!

CLARA: Hold hard, Aniela! Surely, that will do!

ANIELA: It does no harm to take a little care.
(Brief pause.)
And, after this … we'll never love again?

CLARA: Each shall become the sweetheart of her friend …

ANIELA:	*(Pensive.)*
	Each … the other … what a fine example!
	But tell me, Clara … talking about men –
	You're sure their love is *never* quite sincere?
CLARA:	Never?
	(Brief pause.)
	Quite sure …
ANIELA:	Then why do they pretend?
CLARA:	As to the whys and wherefores, I'm not clear,
	But much I've read and well recall this sample:
	"Of all adventures, love's the very worst;
	In case of danger, opt for drowning first!"
ANIELA:	For pity's sake! That's going to excess!
CLARA:	I swear that's what the book advised, no less.
ANIELA:	That being so, it's cause for grief profound
	That all girls fall in love and none is drowned!
CLARA:	Girls are concerned for their soul's salvation.
	They live for heaven, love for tribulation!
ANIELA:	Oh, wicked men!
CLARA:	Hell's portals gave them birth!
ANIELA:	Is there no country free from men on earth?
CLARA:	*(Speaking rapidly.)*
	Take Gustave – that young Warsaw jackanapes!
ANIELA:	Oh, *he* can't be bothered to deceive …
CLARA:	You're honoured if a syllable escapes –
ANIELA:	He'll marry from sheer boredom, I believe –
	At least, I shall be spared his groans and sighs –
CLARA:	I see no point in that! What I advise
	Is punishment … you make him weep and wail!
ANIELA:	If only one could trust a loving male,
	The world would be a happier place for all!
CLARA:	It *was* – some years ago, if you recall
	The books we used to read …

ANIELA: Yes, as a girl …
            The thought of them still puts me in a whirl…

            Enter PANI DOBRUSKA and ALBIN.

DOBRUSKA: *(To ALBIN.)*
            Who quarrels, loves – or so the proverb went…

CLARA: Did Auntie quarrel?

DOBRUSKA: Oh, you innocent!

CLARA: Me?

DOBRUSKA: You!

CLARA: Why?

ANIELA: Come, Mama, agree
            That Clara's very sensible –

CLARA: Aniela equally!

ANIELA: In all things, we see eye to eye –

CLARA: And each of us consults –

DOBRUSKA: I daresay two consulting heads
            Produce desired results –
            But in a mother's house,
            Politeness does no harm
            And nobody will suffer
            By exhibiting some charm!
            So now, perhaps, Aniela
            Cousin Clara will advise
            That, even if indifferent,
            Girls need not despise!

CLARA: *(Curtseying low to ALBIN.)*
            We thank you, Master Albin,
            You've been so very kind!

ANIELA: *(To PANI DOBRUSKA.)*
            Gustave I'm to woo likewise?
            Be at his beck and call?

DOBRUSKA: Don't always look so sulky –
            And please try not to pout!

They sit down round the table. DOBRUSKA and ANIELA take up their sewing, but not CLARA.

ANIELA:	He doesn't even see us!
CLARA:	He might be dumb and blind!
ANIELA:	Am I supposed to humour him?
	To draw the fellow out?
CLARA:	Prattle when he's silent?
	Sparkle when he bores?
ANIELA:	Convince him even country folk
	Know how to give a ball –
CLARA:	*(Same tone, speaking faster still.)*
	And country-girls can talk as well
	As town-bred sophomores?
ANIELA:	Of sun and rainy weather –
	And how the crops have grown!
CLARA:	His townbred wits, of course
	Would far outshine our own!
ANIELA:	To spare us shame, he draws a veil
	Upon his intellect!
CLARA:	And courts us when he's half asleep,
	For pity, I suspect!
DOBRUSKA:	You seem content, my pretty ones,
	Out-talking one another …
ANIELA:	What else are we supposed to do
	To pass the time, dear Mother?
CLARA:	Spreadeagled on the sofa, he's at ease –
	Eyes half-shut and muttering, if you please!
	Should we strike up a merry roundelay
	Or dance about him garlanded with hay?

As she speaks the last line, CLARA – kerchief in hand – sketches a few dance-steps. ALBIN leaps forward and moves a chair, though it's standing well behind her.

ALBIN:	Watch out!

CLARA: What for?

ALBIN: The chair!

CLARA: *(Angrily.)*

                              With you close by,
            A girl can't even stumble –

ALBIN: More's the pity!

ANIELA: *(To PANI DOBRUSKA.)*
            So sensible!

DOBRUSKA: *(Laughing.)*

                    I really wonder why –
            No need to dance a jig or sing them ditties –
            Just be polite and don't show off, my pretties!

CLARA: *(Ironically.)*

            Take Radost, Gustave, Albin – all three males!
            In that triumvirate, *man's* law prevails:
            Being of one mind, what more do they require?
            What could mere female intellect aspire –
            As Heaven's feeblest product – to impart
            To three such wise men, masters of the Earth?
            How could we match their standards for a start?
            Our feelings and our views, despised from birth –
            Since what *men* thought was all that really mattered
            –
            Have always been dismissed as flawed or fettered!

DOBRUSKA: Things are not always quite as they appear:
            Men have their faults – but so have we, my dear!
            Sweet reason's balance tends to favour them
            Who pardon others and themselves condemn!

SCENE TWO

(DOBRUSKA, ANIELA, CLARA, ALBIN, GUSTAVE. ALBIN stands right of stage while the three women are seated at the table, sewing. GUSTAVE enters, bows, places a chair centre stage and sits down, more or less facing the audience. Throughout this scene, GUSTAVE talks absent-mindedly, as though for the sake of talking and is much preoccupied with his clothes.)

GUSTAVE:	I see the rain has stopped. The sky's quite bright…
CLARA:	Delightful weather, really – mild and clear … *(To ANIELA.)* No one could say that I'm not being polite! And now it's up to you, Aniela dear!
DOBRUSKA:	*(To CLARA, sounding displeased.)* Clara! What ails you? *(To GUSTAVE.)* Didn't Albin remark That fresh clouds seem to threaten yet more rain?
ALBIN:	For me, the outlook's gloomy, very dark! Since all my aspirations prove in vain, And Clara merely revels in my grief!
CLARA:	*(Impatiently.)* Far from it! Clara's deeply sympathetic …
GUSTAVE:	*(Abstractly.)* You're busy!
CLARA:	Men may find our tasks pathetic But, nonetheless, they furnish swift relief Where rustic boredom thrives in such profusion.
DOBRUSKA:	*(Sharply, to CLARA.)* *You're* bored?
CLARA:	*Me*, Aunty? No, there's some confusion!
GUSTAVE:	To need relief suggests a person's weak …
CLARA:	Should we forever have ourselves in mind?
GUSTAVE:	*(Glancing towards ALBIN.)* And those close by, that's surely right and proper!

CLARA: *(With mounting irritation.)*

Close or distant – boredom's not unique!

ANIELA: *(To CLARA.)*

Oh Clara, drop it!

GUSTAVE: *(Still indifferent.)*

Best advice, I find –

CLARA: That's welcome!

GUSTAVE: – given to children who've been spoiled…

CLARA: I'll know just where to turn …

GUSTAVE: *(Indifferently.)*

The looking-glass …

DOBRUSKA: Clara gets heated … there's no way to stop her!

Blow on the spark, she's straightaway embroiled!

GUSTAVE: *(Stretching himself in his chair.)*

Pray do not fret! I find her quite diverting!

CLARA: *(Hurt and ironical.)*

That such a miracle should come to pass

Through words of mine … How very disconcerting!

(To ALBIN.)

Could you not bear to free me from your gaze?

ALBIN: *(Sighing.)*

May I not look?

CLARA: There are less steadfast ways,

(Aside to ANIELA.)

I'll pull a face if that would make him blink!

DOBRUSKA: *(After brief pause.)*

Gustave, it may astonish you, I think,

That, at this time of year, our rural calm

For anyone at all should hold much charm.

GUSTAVE: *(Speaking more and more slowly.)*

Not in the least surprised … whatever reason …

The country's …

(Stifling a yawn.)

                    … yes, enchanting at this season!

CLARA: *(Aside to ANIELA.)*
You see?

ANIELA: What?

CLARA: Yawning …

ANIELA: Manners …

CLARA: Aunty's phrase:
(Aloud.)
Manners require …
(Catches a look from PANI DOBRUSKA and quickly changes the sense.)
                    … what you dislike, you praise!

GUSTAVE: *(Gradually slowing down.)*
Country life has got its charms, that's true:
(Stifling a yawn.)
In spring, the flowers come out; the grass is new;
In summer … summer … brings the lovely crops …
In autumn …
(Yawning.)
          something else … it never stops.
And then…those winter evenings…cold, dark nights:
Parties…why, yes…the whole year round…delights!

Doses off.

DOBRUSKA: It's up to us, whether life's dull or fun …
If hours slip idly by, no task begun –
No time devoted to essential chores –
If, amid ceaseless bustle and commotion,
We crave new faces, novelty, emotion,
Then, life at last – in town or country – bores!
And that being so, there's little hope, I fear,
That Master Gustave will enjoy being here!

CLARA: Shush, Aunty!

Points at sleeping GUSTAVE.

He's quite happy –

DOBRUSKA: So it seems!

CLARA: Let's all just go …

ANIELA: … and leave him to his dreams!

ALBIN: And *I* can't sleep at *night*!

DOBRUSKA: This is too much!

CLARA: Come on!

DOBRUSKA: Ah, no!

ANIELA: *(Pulling her my the hand.)*
Mama, make haste!

CLARA: *(Seizing her other hand.)*
I'll second that! Concern for him's misplaced.
He'll not be roused, his weariness is such.
He's made his bed; so let him lie, I say!
*(*Impatiently to *ALBIN.)*
For goodness' sake, come on! Let's creep away!

*Exeunt ALL, leaving GUSTAVE asleep. A few moments later,
RADOST runs in, gazes mournfully at GUSTAVE, wrings his
hands in despair, then sits down in the chair just vacated
by DOBRUSKA.*

RADOST: *(To GUSTAVE, still asleep, speaking in a loud voice on
brink of tears.)*
Gustave, dear boy! You're cruelty's appalling.

GUSTAVE: *(Opens eyes, looks straight ahead and resumes speaking as
if to PANI DOBRUSKA.)*
As I was saying, country life's enthralling!

RADOST: *(Bursts out laughing.)*
I can't help laughing, though you drive me mad!

GUSTAVE: *(Startled, stands up after brief silence.)*
I nodded off –

RADOST: *(Ironical.)*
You did?

GUSTAVE: *(Displeased.)*

Is that so bad?
I fell asleep!

RADOST: Forgive me for recalling:
(Imitating GUSTAVE.)
"Uncle, I'll mend my ways, you'll be astounded".
I am! To find you snoring – I'm dumb-founded!

GUSTAVE: I slept … I'm sorry … but do bear in mind,
No lover's lulled to sleep by cannon's roar,
(Simulating emotion.)
But by the soothing flutes of womankind!

RADOST: Their fluting voices! Come, Gustave, no more!
In heaven's name, God grant me painless death!
All my advice, my pleading – wasted breath!
What ails you? Is your soul bereft of life –
To snore beside a sweetheart, like a wife?

GUSTAVE: *(Displeased with himself, stands up, pushes chair away.)*
Too comfortable by half! The devil's snare!
Sleep overcame me, took me unaware!

RADOST: That's modern courtship for you! Hopes to wed!
If sleep's you want, enjoy it, sleepy-head.

GUSTAVE: I couldn't help it, Uncle! Come, be fair! -

RADOST: The deuce you couldn't! Nor did time allow
For wishing all goodnight and rest in peace!

GUSTAVE: If Uncle, you will please not knit your brow,
I promise all unpleasantness will cease!

RADOST: *(Restraining him.)* How? When? Where?

GUSTAVE: I swear I'll make amends …

RADOST: *(Pleadingly.)*
Don't mock me, Gustave! Think before you speak!
Be sensible for seven days – one week!

GUSTAVE: Two weeks, I promise! Uncle, let's be friends!

RADOST: I'll pray for you!

GUSTAVE: Dear Uncle, that is kind!

I've earned your rage, deserve to be maligned!
Parental guidance nonetheless I treasure:
I'm grateful to you, Uncle, beyond measure!
(They embrace.)

RADOST: *(Deeply moved.)*
Dear Gustave! But … if only I felt sure
Your purpose of amendment would endure!

GUSTAVE: It will! For I'm in love and so will stay:
Henceforth, I'll outdo Albin! You shall see!

RADOST: *(Holding him back as GUSTAVE prepares to leave.)*
No wait! They'll take a change for mockery:
You'll finish up by causing fresh dismay!

GUSTAVE: I'll only sigh once every half an hour;
I'll gaze, I grant you – who'll take that amiss?
But *how* I'll gaze! I know it's in my power …
(Takes RADOST's hand, speaking softly.)
The way my Uncle eyed a certain miss!

RADOST: *(Placing a hand over his mouth.)*
Be quiet, can't you!
(Glancing round.)
Have you lost your mind?

GUSTAVE: The only trouble is that – sad to say –
The girl in question never looks my way!

RADOST: But, Gustave – it's a *wife* you hope to find!
Would you prefer one with a roving eye,
As though on offer to each passer-by?
On one whose stolen glance, whose sigh discreet
Would seem to whisper "I am yours, my sweet"?

GUSTAVE: I want – though I go foolishly about it –

RADOST: Indeed!

GUSTAVE: I want a good wife –

RADOST: Who could doubt it?

GUSTAVE: To me, Aniela's attributes are clear –

(RADOST, in delighted silence, stretches out his hand.)
Or, as I'm sure you know, I'd not be here!

RADOST: *(Hugging him.)*
Is this an angel speaking in your stead?

GUSTAVE: Then, I'm not always such a dunderhead?

RADOST: Alas, my boy, if only it could last …

GUSTAVE: Well, merrily on my way –

RADOST: *(Dolefully, seizing his hand.)*
                              Hold, not so fast!
(GUSTAVE silences him with a hug.)

GUSTAVE: You'll be amazed how I'll improve today!

Inadvertently knocks RADOST's snuff-box from his hand and overturns a chair as he runs from the room. As the curtain falls, RADOST is seen alternatively hunting for the snuff-box and peering after GUSTAVE.

RADOST: Lord have mercy! Gustave! Wait, I say!

END OF ACT ONE

ACT TWO

SCENE ONE

DOBRUSKA and RADOST.

DOBRUSKA: Yes, dear friend, I share your troubled feeling:
Young Master Gustave's ways are unappealing.
Such selfish arrogance, to tell the truth,
I find hard to pardon in a youth …

RADOST: That's not his vice –

DOBRUSKA: Oh, he's a saint, I know!
No faults whatever?

RADOST: Would that it were so!

DOBRUSKA: What, for example?

RADOST: Flippant, lacks discretion –
Frankly, he's fickle –

DOBRUSKA: That's not my impression.

RADOST: But, good Mistress, that much I admit!
He's nonetheless kind-hearted and a wit …
Unlike frivolity, such traits endure.
A wife and children he'll delight, for sure.

DOBRUSKA: You find no fault –

RADOST: I love him like a son!
(Mournfully.)
I'm single, though.

DOBRUSKA: I'm not the guilty one!

RADOST: Aniela's quite upset –

DOBRUSKA: With reason, too!

RADOST: Poor boy! They've really got it in for you!

DOBRUSKA: To fall asleep! Not fickle – just disdainful!

RADOST: I woke him up! …

DOBRUSKA:	I'm much obliged! 'Twas painful!
	Later, he stormed us, like a man possessed!
	You saw him!
RADOST:	Surely, pardonable zest!
DOBRUSKA:	I relish youth's high spirits, if unfeigned;
	Even if they're sometimes unrestrained –
	But when the mood's assumed and sheer pretence –
	Like Gustave's lunacy today – there's no defence!
RADOST:	Yes, he was mad today, beyond all doubt –
	But shyness can occasion such a bout:
	He trembles, stands, then bolts – a restive horse!
	No ditch or hedgerow throws the boy off-course!
	That's Gustave! What's he chasing none can guess –
DOBRUSKA:	*(Trying not to laugh.)*
	You say he's …
RADOST:	Shy –
DOBRUSKA:	What, Gustave?
RADOST:	Shy, no less!
DOBRUSKA:	That's rich!
	(She laughs.)
	Poor little Gussie, helpless mite!
	He's all at sea!
RADOST:	*(Confused.)*
	Bit brash … you may be right …
	(Miserably.)
	What can I do?
DOBRUSKA:	Why, you must take a stand!
	Between ourselves, young Gustave's out of hand.
	Dear Uncle he ignores … does as he like –
RADOST:	No, there you're wrong, ma'am! Every hour that strikes
	I tell him off – a flea in either ear!
DOBRUSKA:	You may well preach – but Gustave doesn't hear.

RADOST: He does – and thanks me for my words of caution.
            You're fond of truth? Let me serve you a portion!
            You spoil those girls of yours in every way!

DOBRUSKA: Spoil?

RADOST: Madam …

DOBRUSKA: I? Not likely!

RADOST: Sad to say!
            A fact …

DOBRUSKA: They quake …

RADOST: *(Ironically.)*
                            No doubt …

DOBRUSKA: That's not my failing!
            Wish you'd been there today to hear them wailing!

RADOST: *I* may not count and Gustave's faults be great:
            At least, he's frank …

DOBRUSKA: Do you insinuate … ?
            Which of them do you mean, or is it both?

RADOST: Ahem!

DOBRUSKA: Well?

RADOST: What of those vows?

DOBRUSKA: Some childish oath!
            I take no notice but the blame I'd lay
            With Clara's home. Aniela used to stay.
            The parents' set a very poor example;
            Unwholesome books the girls would slyly sample,
            And scandals – by my brother-in-law recounted –
            Not in young hearts, but in young heads implanted
            This hatred of men – their latest craze.
            But why heed what is just a passing phase?

RADOST: No doubt they'll change, but Gustave's state is such …

DOBRUSKA: Too little feeling's better than too much!

RADOST: *(Kissing her hand emotionally.)*
            My dear, good lady!

DOBRUSKA: *You've* not changed, that's clear!

RADOST: *(Emotionally, as before.)*
              Never …

DOBRUSKA: Go, coddle that boy …
              (Exit DOBRUSKA.)

RADOST: *(Grimly.)*
                         I will, don't fear!
              (Alone.)
              What am I to do with him?
              I've got to find some way!
              If I could truss him like a ram
              And then by force convey
              The rascal to the altar
              And make him take a wife,
              The pair of them would be assured
              Of happiness for life!
              Instead, capricious as a loach,
              He'll slither, squirm and swivel –
              Stir the mud around as you approach –
              Then hide – the crafty devil!
              (Enter GUSTAVE.)

GUSTAVE: Uncle, how now? Have I not much improved?

RADOST: I'd not believe it, if I hadn't seen!

GUSTAVE: But Annie doesn't help; she's quite unmoved!

RADOST: Birds of a feather! Is that what you mean!

GUSTAVE: She pouts at me …

RADOST: *(To himself.)*
                         Annie? … some progress there …

GUSTAVE: Favours are prized the more for being rare;
              She needn't speak, but let her love be keen!
              My heart is more than ever in her thrall –

FREDRO / CLARKE

RADOST: *(Angrily.)*
               Hers less in yours!

GUSTAVE: Less?

RADOST: Less!

GUSTAVE: Oh, spare me mirth!

RADOST: *(Ironically.)*
               Mirth!

GUSTAVE: Not fair …

RADOST: *(Angrier still.)*
                        It is!

GUSTAVE: Why?

RADOST: All you're worth!

GUSTAVE: What have I done?

RADOST: You've no idea at all?
               Yes gods, you want to send me to my grave?
               I thought a tarantula had nipped your heel –
               In vain my winks and grunts … Would you behave?
               No! Hopped and skipped, like someone at a reel,
               Bumping, breaking! Even the puppy flew!

GUSTAVE: What harm? I merely played a trick or two …

RADOST: Of parlour-tricks, you're master without peer –
               But none requiring grace or skill, I fear!
               A prankster who descends to stupid ploys
               May raise a laugh, but his good name destroys;
               And those his tricks are meant to entertain
               And hurt instead and take him for insane.

GUSTAVE: How true, dear Uncle! You are right to scold!
               I'm fortunate to have you by my side:
               Such clear advice, so competent a guide –
               At time, I am inclined to foolish pranks.

RADOST: *(Raising eyes to heaven.)*
               At times?

GUSTAVE: *(Hugging him.)*

Yes, dearest Uncle – heart of gold! –
For your advice and sermons, deepest thanks!
Your remedies shall be at once applied …

RADOST: *(Imploringly.)*
Now, conversation …

GUSTAVE: That can go to Hades!
May all their throats clog up with barnyard cackle!

RADOST: He's off again!

GUSTAVE: Amusing country ladies
Is an art too fine for town-bred males to tackle!
Mention the great wide world – that's airs and graces!
Talk about farming: "What do you take us for?
Obsessed with pails and pitchforks? You're a bore!"
Try books … You're far too learned … Vacant faces!
Make jokes … You're flippant! Don't … a sobersides!
A sage is arrogant; a clown derides!
When in the country, where you're just a name,
Whatever you say or do, you'll be to blame!

RADOST: Aniela, though, is not like that, I trust?

GUSTAVE: What does one say to her? I've talked of fields,
Of meadows, rivers, fruit, sheep, harvest-yields –
So, what the devil's left to discuss?

RADOST: What ails you? Why invoke the Evil One?
When you're in town …

GUSTAVE: In town, virgins I shun!

RADOST: Virgins or not, whose taste is that refined?

GUSTAVE: My dear good Uncle, you've become so old!
Were I afraid to speak my ardent mind,
I'd twist and turn each word a hundred-fold,
Before the goal I sought was slowly gained:
Thoughts, like water, rise the more constrained!

RADOST: Sound reasoning, the simile is nice …

GUSTAVE: For any maiden, should it not suffice

To breathe "I love you"? She, in affirmation,
Then whispers: "I love *you*"? Hang conversation!

RADOST: And if she doesn't?

GUSTAVE: That, too, is the end …

RADOST: Of you as well – your aspirations dead!
But hold your horses! Steady on, my friend!
You know what Aniela and Clara have agreed?

GUSTAVE: No … what?

RADOST: That they'll stay single … never wed!

GUSTAVE: *(Pretending horror, takes him aside.)*
I don't believe it! Never wed, indeed!
Renounce all men and virtuous remain?
Like women everywhere?

RADOST: *(Chucking him under the chin.)*
              Hush, scatterbrain!
(Exit RADOST.)

GUSTAVE: *(Alone, after a short silence.)*
So chill a glance and yet – a loving eye!
Locked in her bosom, so profound a sigh!
She smiles and yet her brow is knit with care …
I'm bitten, smitten – madly in love, I swear!

Enter ANIELA and CLARA. ANIELA sits down with her needlework. GUSTAVE makes a point of addressing all his remarks to her. When speaking to ANIELA, his tone is endearing. To CLARA he speaks sarcastically or with contemptuous indifference. CLARA talks rapidly and vehement often instead of ANIELA who speaks slowly and gently as the scenes that follow.

After a long war, armistice ensues.

ANIELA: I ask for peace –

GUSTAVE: And who could peace refuse?

CLARA: *(Standing between them.)*
Not all deserve it!

136

GUSTAVE: *(Ignoring CLARA.)*

                              What's the first condition?

CLARA: Come, not so fast!

GUSTAVE: Why, mutual recognition!

ANIELA: I shall be neutral ...

GUSTAVE: No, you cannot be!

              Let's rather sign a non-aggression treaty!

CLARA: How splendid!

GUSTAVE: Now, the clauses – one, two, three!

ANIELA: You're joking!

GUSTAVE: No ... I'm pleading ...

CLARA: *(Ironic.)*

                              Some entreaty!

GUSTAVE: What?

CLARA: My advice ...

GUSTAVE: I beg ...

CLARA: *(Angry aside.)*

                              I s'pose he sees me!

GUSTAVE: I swear I'll faithfully ...

CLARA: *(Aside.)*   He's out to tease me!

GUSTAVE: I swear twice over ...

CLARA: He who begs for trust

              Signs what he must ...

GUSTAVE: *(Indifferently, not looking at her.)*

                              The hapless beggar may

              Find treasure ...

CLARA: He will walk a long, long way!

GUSTAVE: Distance won't shrink his hope or quench his ardour.

CLARA: Conquest is hard ...

GUSTAVE: *(Looking her in the eye; voice cool.)*

                              Humility still harder!

CLARA: *(Heatedly.)* Then war it is!

GUSTAVE:	I'm armed against you, miss!
ANIELA:	I stand by Clara …
GUSTAVE:	How I envy her!
CLARA:	I'm with Aniela …
GUSTAVE:	Why then, war shall cease!
CLARA:	*(With mounting agitation.)* Why should it?
GUSTAVE:	*(Indifferently.)* Why? Since I'm a man of peace – Though less a male pursuit, than maiden's due.
CLARA:	*(Heatedly.)* No! Honesty is something men eschew. Their heart's intent they always try to bluster: Between two lamps, man cowers in the middle!
GUSTAVE:	Why such a lamentable view of men?
CLARA:	It flatters them, I'd say …
GUSTAVE:	*(Ironically.)* A teasing riddle – Whose explanation's quite beyond my ken.
CLARA:	Seduction and betrayal are the arts Man favours most. His trophies – broken hearts! The more his victims and the more he lies, The more renown his wins with every prize!
GUSTAVE:	Hmm, you have my keenest sympathy …
CLARA:	I'm deeply grateful but I fail to see Why you extend it. Please explain the reason.
GUSTAVE:	Because, it seems, you've suffered by man's treason – Although so young in years, so innocent!
CLARA:	Who says I have? That wasn't what I meant.
GUSTAVE:	Poverty, sickness, health – who can describe? Wealth and betrayal, too – without a taste? Mere commonsense discounts a diatribe Culled from a book or two, absorbed in haste.

ANIELA: Still, one or two examples do explain …

GUSTAVE: *(Aiming at CLARA.)*
             As for examples, there are good and bad –
             It's usually the latter we retain.
             (To CLARA.)
             In seeking to avenge all women, sad
             That lovely Clara should have pledged her word
             To honour no admirer with her hand …

CLARA: *(Aroused.)*
             Who told you that?

GUSTAVE: Why, Albin …

CLARA: So, you've heard!
             No doubt a similar communiqué is planned
             Concerning cousin Aniela's vow,
             Since men are always keen to share defeat!

GUSTAVE: *(Hiding annoyance with a laugh.)*
             Miss Clara fights with manly zeal! How sweet!
             That ardour's rosy flush on cheek and brow,
             Reminds me of those Amazons of yore!

CLARA: *(Heatedly.)*
             Ardour – yes, ardour! As I've said before
             And shall repeat a hundred times with pride:
             Men I can't stand! Men I can't abide!
             I've sworn to hate them till the end of time:
             Once more, I pledge to keep that vow sublime!

             (Exit CLARA.)

GUSTAVE: *(As though talking to CLARA.)*
             You'll keep that vow, will you? Just wait and see!
             "To hate all men" … "Sublime", the word you used?
             (To ANIELA.)
             Aniela, you would surely disagree?
             'Twas God who, punishing Man's first offence,
             His heart with the ability to hate infused.

But how could you, the soul of innocence,
Share the minutest particle of blame?
Oh, tell me that you do not feel the same –
That you believe in love, both true and strong!
Evil enough waits with experience:
The prickly thorns of sceptical mistrust
In life's slow-garnered bouquet may belong,
To be accepted in old-age, if so they must;
Pure-hearted faith, however, is youth's flower …

ANIELA: Which fickle wind may pluck within the hour!

GUSTAVE: But once the wind has tugged the blossom free,
The fruit can grow … End of analogy!
(Draws up a chair and sits down. Brief pause.)
I have done nothing to deserve your hate …
Anger, perhaps …

ANIELA: *(Indifferent, preoccupied with sewing throughout.)*
Not mine!

GUSTAVE: Yes, yours!

ANIELA: Not to my knowledge …

GUSTAVE: I'd appreciate
Your pardoning one the folly he abhors …

ANIELA: What's it to do with me?

GUSTAVE: How can you doubt … ?
Whose judgment would I worry more about?
I've sinned …

ANIELA: You have?

GUSTAVE: And I confess …

ANIELA: *(Still indifferent.)*
Well, then?

GUSTAVE: *(Edging closer.)*
Forgive me!

ANIELA: Very well …

GUSTAVE: *(Kissing her hand.)*

	Amen?
ANIELA:	Amen!
GUSTAVE:	From now on, I will act quite otherwise …
	But let Aniela my resolve reward –
	Some hope of future happiness accord!
ANIELA:	I can't …
GUSTAVE:	*(Imploringly.)*
	The merest hope of hope, I'd prize!
ANIELA:	I've none to offer!
GUSTAVE:	*(Starting back in his chair.)*
	Heartless beyond measure!
	(Short pause.)
	Are you acquainted with my Uncle's aim?
ANIELA:	I am …
GUSTAVE:	You know your mother feels the same?
ANIELA:	I do …
GUSTAVE:	Yet will Aniela not bestow
	Her blessing on our dearest wishes?
ANIELA:	No!
GUSTAVE:	*(Leaping to his feet.)*
	No?
ANIELA:	*(Calmly.)*
	No …
GUSTAVE:	*(Ironically.)*
	Short and sweet …
ANIELA:	But frank …
GUSTAVE:	A pleasure!
	(Leaning on the arm of the chair on which he was sitting.)
	Is it those vows?
ANIELA:	It's no good asking *me*!
GUSTAVE:	You'll never wed?
ANIELA:	Not now …
GUSTAVE:	Later, maybe?

ANIELA: The future, who can guess … ?

GUSTAVE: *(Taking a few strides, talking heatedly.)*
                         Why can't one guess?
By all means, guess! The guessing isn't hard!
Soon, with a crash, bang, rattle, we shall see
Some gallant suitor prancing in the yard;
What I'm denied, tomorrow he'll possess!
Is that the way of it?

ANIELA: An open question …

GUSTAVE: *(Sits down again, speaks gently.)*
Permit me, then, to make a small suggestion:
If loath, don't raise my hopes against your will,
But neither let a brusque dismissal kill
All hope, I beg …

ANIELA: I don't quite understand …

GUSTAVE: *(Driven to impatience.)*
You don't quite understand … what does that mean?
Don't want to?

ANIELA: That's another open question!

GUSTAVE: *(Jumps up, walks a few paces.)*
Open question! Damn it! That's absurd!
So are all questions, until the answer's heard.
Maybe I lack those graces which commend,
And someone more like Albin, living near –
Some melancholy swain of aspect drear,
Sighing a thousand times, will win the prize!
(Brief pause; having calmed down, he sits.)
Am I so hateful in Aniela's eyes?

ANIELA: *(Still indifferent, without looking at him.)*
How so?

GUSTAVE: *(Sliding his chair forward.)*
                    Well, am I not?

ANIELA: No.

GUSTAVE: True?

ANIELA: Yes, true!

GUSTAVE: *(Moving chair still closer.)*
              You might look up!

ANIELA: *(Looks up fleetingly, then resumes sewing.)*
                          I did …

GUSTAVE: Yes?

ANIELA: Won't that do?

GUSTAVE: So icy cold!

ANIELA: And how else should I be?

GUSTAVE: *(Heatedly.)*
              At least be angry… Vent your rage on me!

ANIELA: Why rage?

GUSTAVE: *(Jumps up, then, to himself.)*
                          Oh, this is more than I can bear!
              (Takes a few paces, stands in front of her.)
              Is it such fun to hurt me … so amusing
              To make me suffer?

ANIELA: Suffering are you? Where?

GUSTAVE: Can you not credit I'm in love with you?

ANIELA: I can't …

GUSTAVE: *(Sitting down again.)*
              Then let me prove it to you at your choosing …
              Just tell me *how*! Whatever it is, I'll do
              Your bidding …

ANIELA: That's enough! I'm not impressed!

GUSTAVE: *(Wanting to leave but restraining himself with an effort
              and speaking with suppressed anger.)*
              No?

ANIELA: No!

GUSTAVE: May I not speak?

ANIELA: No!

GUSTAVE: Now?

143

ANIELA:	Or ever!
GUSTAVE:	*(Jumps up violently, then, ironical.)*

GUSTAVE: *(Jumps up violently, then, ironical.)*
Surely commands more merciful were never
Heard, nor so congenially expressed!
(Takes a few paces.)
Love, but be silent! Marvellous!   Quite splendid!
In silence love … until my days are ended!
(Briefly silent, then pauses in front of her.)
What prompted this aversion, in God's name?
I'll try to lessen it, if I'm to blame …
At least enlighten me, for what it's worth!

ANIELA: I'm not averse to anyone on earth.

GUSTAVE: Love is no easy option from the start,
But hate is harder still to cultivate.
Today, I am its target, sore at heart –
A specimen for you to contemplate!

ANIELA: Let's drop the subject! Nothing more to say …

GUSTAVE: Easy to bid; beyond me to obey!
(With mounting passion.)
Hear me, Aniela! Listen to the voice
Of one who trusts his future to your choice –
(ANIELA rises.)
Who bares his soul, before his idol stands –
His joys and sorrows placing in your hands!
Weigh them upon your scales with utmost care!
(Trying to restrain her as she leaves.)
My sentiments I don't demand you share –
What heart alone bestows, man cannot claim –
But don't despise my less pretentious aim;
Don't spurn the pains, the efforts I devote
With which true love seeks only to promote
A cherished goal today beyond my reach –
Show me salvation's highway, I beseech!
(Holding her back.)

144

What, you forsake me now without a word?
(Seizing her and speaking vehemently.)
That which no wretch, in misery unheard,
Should claim in vain from her he must adore –
(He kneels down.)
Pity! Your pity – kneeling – I implore!

Exit ANIELA by right rear door. GUSTAVE remains kneeling, facing audience and shaking his head, as much to say "I'm wasting my time". CLARA enters through the door left and GUSTAVE rises hurriedly at the sound of her voice.

CLARA: She's left you doing penance for presumption –
          Or giving thanks for favours you received?

GUSTAVE: Shrewd guesswork, Clara, but a false assumption!
          I'm tired of sitting, walking to and fro –
          So knelt …

CLARA: You don't expect to be believed?
          I'll tell you what transpired, as well I know.
          Your melancholy glances weren't observed;
          Your sentimental sighs no purpose served;
          Your words she scorned – so, what was left for you?
          To kneel and vow to die! In such a stew,
          You need a sword, a dirk, a butcher's steel –
          A suicidal scissors would have done!
          (She laughs.)
          So here we stand and neither speak nor feel?
          Such progress – and the battle scarce begun!
          A victory, though, too easily obtained:
          I'm more surprised than happy it's been gained!

GUSTAVE: My quiver's empty … I'll make no pretence
          Of badinage! You see me in despair …

CLARA: *I* can still find an arrow for defence!
          Joking apart, why such a hangdog air?
          Was it this morning's interrupted sleep,
          Or have you overtaxed your wit's resource?

GUSTAVE: My heart is troubled by dismay so deep,
           My sins I judge so harshly that, perforce,
           I've lost the knack of witty repartee.
           The goal of my desires – once close to me –
           Is now, alas, as good as out of sight …
           My soul's in torment, bitterly aware
           That my mistakes have cost me love's delight!
           What's more, I must admit: it's only fair!
           Condemn my fickleness, as well you may –
           The arrogance that buoyed my hopes so high;
           Censure me for the stupid pranks I play;
           My boorishness – that, too, I'll not deny!
           Scold me as you see fit, the words you choose
           Will be less harsh than I myself would use!

CLARA: *(Feigning humility.)*
           Man's wits so frequently surpass our own –
           As my experience, alas, has shown –
           I'll not presume your judgment to assail …
           If noble Man in reason's honest scale
           Is modestly disposed his faults to weigh,
           I can but echo him, or silent stay!
           This laudable remorse and sad confession –
           Were prompted by what terrible transgression?

GUSTAVE: I know Aniela now … Her views I've heard!

CLARA: But how does that account for your depression?

GUSTAVE: I realise how grievously I erred!

CLARA: *(Pensively.)*
           So, Master Gustave loves her now for sure?

GUSTAVE: I worship her – without exaggeration!

CLARA: *(Deliberately.)*
           Not just a fickle whim that won't endure?

GUSTAVE: The purest, strongest love in all Creation!

CLARA: But will it last, this love you say you feel?

GUSTAVE: As long as life itself will last, I swear!

CLARA:	Aniela, doubtless, thought it wasn't real?
GUSTAVE:	She wouldn't listen … Witness my despair!
CLARA:	*(After short pause.)*
	Too bad! Who knows, were *I* to speak, she might –
GUSTAVE:	Where love dare not, might friendship intercede?
CLARA:	If told how much you've changed and how contrite…
GUSTAVE:	Miss Clara, you have read my thoughts indeed!
CLARA:	I'll speak about your former disposition …
GUSTAVE:	Lay it on thick and no allowance make!
CLARA:	Carefree, like any youth in your position …
GUSTAVE:	A fickle, feckless, absent-minded rake!
CLARA:	Arrogant, wicked, self-absorbed and giddy!
GUSTAVE:	*(Reflecting.)*
	That's over-doing it – a shade too black!
CLARA:	*(Carried away despite herself.)*
	You took Aniela for some country biddy –
GUSTAVE:	Don't go too far!
CLARA:	Assuming in your pride,
	Manners are something country-folk deride!
GUSTAVE:	Too strong!
CLARA:	Devoid of common-sense, which lack …
GUSTAVE:	Come, that's too much! We must keep some perspective!
CLARA:	*(Suddenly adopting mild tone and smiling.)*
	I'll use bold colours, sparing no invective –
	But, on the other hand, take care to stress
	That you've repented, undergone a cure:
	The noble love for her you now profess,
	If slow to bloom, the longer will endure.
	And if, as yet, it cannot be returned,
	It may be trusted and should not be spurned!
GUSTAVE:	My dear Miss Clara, that is so well said!
	We think alike; my inmost thoughts you've read!

CLARA: *(Bursts out laughing.)*
I can't contain myself a moment longer!
"My dear Miss Clara" – His! What impudence!
I've found the right approach and I'm the stronger –
His sword is broken, shattered his defence!
(Seriously.)
Why should male cunning fill our hearts with dread?
Let's rather fear our feeble selves instead;
None but a wilful weakling would deny
(Referring to GUSTAVE.)
That Man's not hard to vanquish, if you try!
Open your heart to him and, no mistake,
He's venomous and nimble as a snake!
Oppose his will, make bold to speak your mind –
A raging lion, a tiger you will find!
However, just play second to his chime –
Pretend to be defeated every time –
And you'll have found the way to get around him
When, not with chains but silk, you've bound him!
I could be wrong, but this day's exercise
Alters my deep conviction in no wise:
So, having voiced my thinking, frank and fervent –
(Curtseying low.)
I'm honoured to remain … your humble servant!
(Exit CLARA by side door right.)

GUSTAVE: *(Alone. Since CLARA's outburst of laughter, he's been
standing as though rooted to the spot.)*
I see … That's how it is … My love's sincere –
Trusting to truth, I make my feelings clear
And here I am – struck down, you salamander,
By twisted reasoning and bitter slander!
I'll not be paired with Albin, no indeed!
You want deceit and subterfuge? … Agreed!
(Takes a few paces deep in thought.)
Aniela's kind, if bound by prejudice …

But lack of trust may yield to kindliness:
I'll fake a romance – and in her confide,
Make her my friend and win her to my side,
Enlist her pity … summon her protection …
(Short silence.)
A secret shared encourages affection.
Desire, by love's portrayal once aroused,
I'll focus on myself till we're espoused …
(Takes a few paces, deep in thought. A silent interlude during which he is obviously hatching a plot. He sits down, jumps up, walks to and fro, then stands still for a moment or two, musing. When he speak, he does so more rapidly than usual, as though releasing a pent-up flow of words. He hardly notices ALBIN who appears in the doorway, pauses in surprise, then slowly approaches.)
Here's Albin, mischief's root and cause,
Like some distressful shade,
Sighing with every breath he draws –
Tears his stock-in-trade!
For fifty years, he's sobbed and groaned;
For fifty years, he sighed and moaned:
No wonder, faced with such a show,
That girls assume love must be so!
As if man lived a hundred years –
To sigh his way through half, in tears!
Weeping and wailing, night and day,
You're like a walking water-works –
Leaving me, when you're away,
To tolerate your Clara's quirks!
Don't love her so submissively –
Then, maybe, some reward you'll see …
Don't let her rule you like a queen,
And she'll obey you, if she can.
Don't bore with tears and woeful mien,
But dominate her! Be a man!

Madness to court a girl your way!
Farewell!
(Adding quietly, as he walks off.)
God keep you ... far away!
(Suddenly turning back for a moment.)
Where did she go?

ALBIN: Who?

GUSTAVE: *(With a shrug.)*

Even that's beyond him!
(Exit GUSTAVE in search of ANIELA.)

ALBIN: He's in a towering rage! How did I wound him?
Where shall I leave my sighs, where shed my tears?
I'll burn with love – two, ten, a hundred years!
If Clara'd glance my way, how could she fail –
Catching the merest glimpse of me – to wail!

Enter CLARA who makes her way to the table and resumes needlework.

Will not the day soon dawn, in tear-dry calm,
And my sore-wounded heart be offered balm?

CLARA: Maybe it will, but I shall not anoint!

ALBIN: I love you!

CLARA: I know ...

ALBIN: I'll wait ...

CLARA: No thanks. No point.

ALBIN: I beg ...

CLARA: Enough of that!

ALBIN: You're cruel!

CLARA: So be it!

ALBIN: Would I might cease to love ...

CLARA: ... That I might see it!

CLARA drops a ball of wool. ALBIN darts to retrieve it.

If I could drop my wool upon the ground

	Without your honour fussing till it's found!
	If once my shawl could slither from the table
	Without your honour squirming on the floor!
	If to seek knife or scissors I were able
	Without your honour fetching them before!
	If, just for once, I might discreetly sneeze
	Without "Long life!" and suchlike auguries!
	I swear it's more than flesh and blood can stand!
ALBIN:	If I anticipate your wish and your command
	And long to dedicate my life to you –
	Ascribe it to a love which is your due!
	To melt your heart I've made vain attempt,
	But tell me, Clara, how I've earned contempt!
CLARA:	Contempt? No, that most certainly it's not!
ALBIN:	But if it's not contempt, then it is – what?
CLARA:	Often I've grieved to see you suffer so.
	It makes no difference … You're sincere, I know,
	But Clara no man's yearning will fulfil:
	I've sworn to hate all men – and that I will!
ALBIN:	Of that fierce hatred, mine is no small share!
CLARA:	Far from the largest …
ALBIN:	Were you but aware
	What havoc in my soul your glances wreak,
	You'd surely grant the happiness I seek …
CLARA:	Oh no, I wouldn't!
ALBIN:	Never?
CLARA:	Save your breath!
ALBIN:	Your words are lethal –
CLARA:	*(Laughing.)* Now I've caused a death!
ALBIN:	The world will soon applaud your grim success!
CLARA:	No man yet died of love, you must confess!
ALBIN:	Maybe none could, but many longed to perish …
CLARA:	Taking as fact, this wish so many cherish,

To mark the death of – Albin, let us say,
Strict mourning I'll observe, as from today!

ALBIN: Ah, Gustave gave me such superb advice!

CLARA: *(Ironically.)*
Your counsellor advised, did he? How nice!

ALBIN speaks slowly, CLARA quickly.

ALBIN: He said, "Don't love so warmly, she'll respond" –

CLARA: "Don't love?" For that upsets him, don't you see?
If someone's loyal, and happy so to be,
His inclination is to snap the band!

ALBIN: He said I'd wept two years, not knowing why –

CLARA: As if you didn't know! A blatant lie!

ALBIN: He said girls like long penance to impose –

CLARA: He'd rather an hour or a minute, I suppose!

ALBIN: "Don't let yourself be ruled" –

CLARA: Upon my word!
"Don't *let* yourself!" Why, that's the best I've heard!

ALBIN: "But you rule her …"

CLARA: What's that? You're being fooled!
Rule right away? Is that your aspiration?
And who could vouch for order in the nation
If one man led a hundred more astray,
Proclaiming "Never let yourself be ruled!"

ALBIN: I won't obey him! I'll do what you say!

CLARA: *(To herself.)* Some counsellor!

ALBIN: *(Approaches her with emotion.)*
What shall I do?

CLARA: JUST GO AWAY!
(ALBIN bows, sighs deeply and departs.)
Speak! Be silent! Come! Go! Turn or twist!
And he obeys! If only he'd resist!

His weak-kneed readiness to bow to fate
Makes him impossible to love or hate!

END OF ACT TWO

ACT THREE

SCENE ONE

Enter ANIELA, followed by GUSTAVE, through door right.

GUSTAVE: Aniela, please! I crave a final word.

ANIELA: There seems no end of final words today!
But just to save repeating all you've heard,
Let me assure you, Gustave, once for all:
To every man, whatever may befall,
The same point-blank refusal I'll convey,
As earlier upon yourself conferred
To honour my commitment. But I stress
There's nothing personal in my decision.
Although I can't diminish your distress,
I trust you will observe just one provision:
I'd like to hope my answer will be treated
In strictest confidence and not repeated.
I'm contravening my Mama's decree:
Love's traps are obvious, she would agree,
Yet may in time ensnare if caution's lacking;
So my intent she bade me not betray,
But patiently to note what suitors say:
And know the man, before I send him packing.

GUSTAVE: Your wish to act straightforwardly I share.
Despite my Uncle's very strict injunction,
I'll bare my heart to you without compunction:
I love –

ANIELA: How many times I've heard that said!

GUSTAVE: Yes, but – Aniela, please – it isn't you!
(After short silence.)
Since there's no clash of will between us two,
You have become my only hope instead.

No wonder you're astonished! It is a fact!
My Uncle reared me, since both parents lacked –
Steering my fate well-nigh since cradle-days –
Kind and considerate in all sorts of ways!
But, finally, he wanted some reward –
And what a one, ye gods! I begged, I cried …
All means to gain his sympathy, I tried
In vain! My pleas for mercy he ignored.
He finally persuaded me to yield –
And seek your hand regardless of my heart!
Today, when headstrong passion I revealed –
With trembling lips my longing did impart –
I must confess – are you not moved to hear? –
My heart was secretly a prey to fear …

ANIELA: Fear? But of what?

GUSTAVE: Unhappily, 'twas so …
Your charm and virtues which I've come to know,
Daily discovering some fresh attribute
Which only you would modestly dispute –
All that, for someone else, would spell delight
Filled me instead with overpowering fright!
To win a friendly glance, to earn your smile –
Affection's first faith longing to beguile –
Not joy, not glory – heaven, that must be!
Yet fear besets me … and not only me!

ANIELA: You love another, if I've understood …

GUSTAVE: How else could your attraction be withstood?
I was in love already, when we met:
Thence my ambivalent behaviour stemmed,
Which you quite understandably condemned.
I thought you right, admitting with regret
That I, though innocent, was still to blame.
Would you, Aniela, not have felt the same?

ANIELA: In such a quandary, I'd make bold to say,
Telling your Uncle is the only way
To solve the problem –

GUSTAVE: If you knew how often
I'd fallen at his feet with tearful plea,
Admitting all, deploring his decree …

ANIELA: What does he say?

GUSTAVE: My Uncle will not soften.
He just insists that you must be my wife!
You won't be – less aversion than abstention –
But my true heart's desire – love of my life –
He won't allow me to so much as mention!

ANIELA: Why ever not?

GUSTAVE: It's very complicated:
In short, the whole affair originated
With a long-standing row – a duel rather –
Between my Uncle and Aniela's father …

ANIELA: Aniela's father?

GUSTAVE: Yes, you share her name –
Whose echo, gently throbbing in my brain,
A sweet disorder seemed to set in train,
So when I met you and already missed her –
I felt for you, as though you were her sister!

ANIELA: Strange!

GUSTAVE: If pangs of love could be restricted
To one's own self, instead of being inflicted!
But knowing that the pain one undergoes,
Is duplicated in another's throes –
By her who is to me than life more dear –
That's torment, Aniela, without peer!
I'm sorely tempted now life to relinquish –
And thereby mutual agony extinguish!

ANIELA: *(Frightened, close to tears.)*
Gustave, what's that you say? You'd surely never

156

Decide to kill yourself! That's no solution –
But mortal sin – a crime whose execution
Condemns the suicide to hell for ever!

Rapid exchange between them.

GUSTAVE: Then, save me!

ANIELA: That I will, if you'll allow –

GUSTAVE: You can –

ANIELA: And there'll be no more talk of death?

GUSTAVE: No …

ANIELA: I'm shuddering still! Quite out of breath!

GUSTAVE: Then you will help?

ANIELA: But what … ?

GUSTAVE: I'll tell you how!
Prevail upon your mother …

ANIELA: I'll prevail!

GUSTAVE: To pardon me –

ANIELA: She'll pardon, I feel sure!

GUSTAVE: Beg –

ANIELA: I'll implore, beseech, weep, plead, make sure
She gives us her assistance without fail!
Take heart, Gustave – despair's of no avail!

GUSTAVE: My life and happiness I trust to you!

ANIELA: To me? Oh, Lord!

GUSTAVE: Your mother you'll persuade …

ANIELA: I will … I will … you needn't be afraid;
But, in the last resort, what can she do?

GUSTAVE: She'll get round Uncle …

ANIELA: *(Happily.)*
               Clever … no mistake!
I'll talk to her at once; a life's at stake!

GUSTAVE: Heavens! Not yet! Your mother might begin
Accusing Uncle of a major sin

For hazarding your happiness in life,
By forcing me to seek you for my wife.
Their friendship wrecked by inter-family strife,
Where could I hide, my hapless self to save
From twofold enmity, but in the grave?

ANIELA: What's to be done?

GUSTAVE: You want to help?

ANIELA: Why, yes!

GUSTAVE: Then, as we both are now, let us remain:
I seemingly still deep in love with you –
While you complete indifference profess …
Then, later, when they make their purpose plain,
I'll clearly state my eagerness to woo.
You will reject me – loudly, in full view.
That should accord with your dear mother's wishes;
Uncle, although doubtless angry and suspicious,
At least can't say that I've disobeyed him!
Not till then, shall I enlist your help:
Then, you can beg your mother to persuade him.

ANIELA: Ah, now I understand …

GUSTAVE: *(Kisses her hand.)*
No longer hating?

ANIELA: The happy outcome of our plan awaiting!

GUSTAVE: Never forget, brave as you are and just,
My confidence in you, my total trust!
Should you forsake me in my hour of need,
I've nobody but you to intercede.
On your support, protectress and friend,
My hopes of future happiness depend.
Should, thanks to you, Aniela be my wife,
I'll not have time enough, nor span of life
To recompense the kindness you have shown!
Unworthy I may be, but I'll atone!

He kisses her hand with emotion. Enter RADOST unseen, just in time to hear the last line, at which he clasps his hands approvingly.

ANIELA: He heard?

GUSTAVE: Heard what?

RADOST: Well done, my dears! Bravo!

GUSTAVE: *(Going down on one knee before RADOST.)*
Forgive me!

RADOST: *(Starting back in surprise.)*
Why? This is a great delight!

GUSTAVE: *(Moves behind him, speaking quietly.)*
If you *did* hear, upbraid me! Let me know!

RADOST: Gustave!

GUSTAVE: *(Softly.)*
Be furious!
(Loudly.)
Pity on my plight!
(Starts back as if struck by RADOST.)
No need for violence to refuse me!
(Low voice.)
Be angry, Uncle! Make a show! Abuse me!

RADOST: Listen, you fool!

GUSTAVE: *(Low voice.)*
Behave as if you meant it!

RADOST: Have you gone mad?

GUSTAVE: *(Low voice.)*
That's it!
(Loud.)
I'm quite demented!

RADOST: On top of everything!

GUSTAVE: *(Loud.)*
I've told her all!
(Low voice.)

	Come, Uncle! Much more fiery – show some gall!
RADOST:	Oh, go to hell!
GUSTAVE:	*(Low voice.)*
	That's it!
RADOST:	You're mocking me!
GUSTAVE:	*(Aloud in tragic tone of voice.)*
	Uncle, you mean to bury me, I see!
RADOST:	*(Angry.)*
	You've jested long enough, my dear young sir!
	Do what you like and let what may occur!
	I'll help no lunatic to find a mate –
	(On his way out.)
	You're clearly raving mad, you addlepate!

Exit RADOST.

ANIELA:	*(Uneasily.)*
	What now?
GUSTAVE:	*(Quietly.)*
	I know my knees are devilish sore!
ANIELA:	He'd not relent?
GUSTAVE:	As stubborn as before!
ANIELA:	Perhaps he didn't hear?
GUSTAVE:	You mean?
ANIELA:	Maybe –
GUSTAVE:	You said yourself …
ANIELA:	Why no, I merely wondered …
GUSTAVE:	If not, that tiff was pointless and I blundered …
	'Twas very badly timed, if you ask me!
	I'm almost certain he didn't hear,
	But now he'll not take long to realize …
ANIELA:	Everything ruined by untimely passion!
GUSTAVE:	He just slunk in and took me by surprise …

ANIELA:	*(Pacing to and fro uneasily.)*
	What I can do to help is far from clear …
GUSTAVE:	*(Aside.)*
	To let him guess my plan in such a fashion!
ANIELA:	*(Still pacing.)*
	How was it possible your vehemence
	Could wreck our carefully considered plot?
	Your poor Aniela's pain will be intense!
GUSTAVE:	*(Taking her hand.)*
	How could one know the girl and love her not?
ANIELA:	Love her one must …
GUSTAVE:	And so I've sworn to do.
ANIELA:	That I can well believe.
GUSTAVE:	That's all I crave!
	So, you *do* see, I'm sure; I count on you –
	My only source of help, my hope unique!
ANIELA:	But why? What matter now how I behave …
	Your once-kind Uncle his revenge will seek?
GUSTAVE:	But if he didn't hear, I'll put things straight –
ANIELA:	Then do so, Gustave – right away, don't wait!
GUSTAVE:	Meanwhile, whatever else, take care
	Not to converse with him; instead, let's try
	To meet here and discuss the whole affair
	In further detail later – you and I!
	(Taking her hand.)
	And I entreat you, always bear in mind:
	To your safe hands my future I've consigned –
	What's more – the joy of Aniela's heart,
	From which no power on earth my own shall part!

Kisses her hand a few times, walks towards the door of his room and, after taking a quick look round, leaves by another door.

ANIELA: *(Alone, paces deep in thought, then sits, resting head on hand.)*

Strange how his words are ringing in my ear …
Such words addressed to me, I've yet to hear!
He really loves her; not the slightest doubt!
All that he says, his honest gaze bears out.
Happy she'll be with him and he with her;
What more is needed, rapture to confer?
One word – that's all – to seal their happiness –
Or rather bliss! Sheer heaven, at a guess!
They trust each other, love with such persistence!
Am I happier for denying love's existence?
That love's a fact and lasts: that much is proved!
How could I have a heart and not be moved?

Enter CLARA.

CLARA: So rapt in contemplation? Writing a book?

ANIELA: Oh, Clara, Clara! If you only knew!
I'll tell you all … Our friendship will not brook
Betrayal, so my secret's safe with you:
It's Aniela Gustave loves – not me!

CLARA: He loves?

ANIELA: Aniela! But his Uncle won't agree.
Strictly between ourselves! Don't breathe a word!

CLARA: I'm lost …

ANIELA: But I've already made too free!

CLARA: What?

ANIELA: Rancour, hate, pig-headedness unheard!

CLARA: *(Mounting impatience.)*
Who?

ANIELA: Radost –

CLARA: Against … ?

ANIELA: Her! Can you not see?

CLARA: But who … ?

162

ANIELA: So far as I'm concerned, don't worry!
              I'm not the girl that Gustave wants to marry …

CLARA: Too bad! All men should be compelled to languish,
           To teach them how we women scorn the breed –
           Including Gustave! Lectures on how to rule!

ANIELA: Poor Gustave!

CLARA: *(Ironically.)*
                    Poor?

ANIELA: He may have played the fool …

CLARA: I see he's touched you with his show of anguish.

ANIELA: Oh no! I hate all men … I do indeed!
           But Gustave's fate, his future, to protect
           I've promised …

CLARA: …promised gladly, I suspect!

ANIELA: Gladly or not, I can't betray his trust.

CLARA: Betray him! Yes, betray the sultan's whim!

ANIELA: I'll not play false!

CLARA: I'll help … Betray you *must*!

ANIELA: He loves Aniela truly – and she him!

CLARA: I'm lost again!

ANIELA: Wait! I'll explain it all …

CLARA: *(Curious.)*
           Tell me!

ANIELA: Where's Mama?

CLARA: I heard her call –

ANIELA: She's kind and good, in her, I can confide –
           But no one else, just yet … I'd better not!

CLARA: Aniela dear, may God your footsteps guide
           And keep you safe from Man's perfidious plot!
           I fear your hate grows weaker – and your will!

ANIELA: Oh no! As I love you, I hate men still!

           (Enter RADOST, as girls prepare to leave.)

RADOST: Miss Aniela!

ANIELA seizes CLARA by the hand and pulls her towards side-door right; they run out quickly.

Come, Miss! Here, what's wrong?
(RADOST starts to follow them but turns back.)
They're scared of me! That's Gustave – stake my eye!
I'll bet he's got a finger in this pie!
Gustave, I'll see you frightened stiff ere long!
(Enter GUSTAVE through one of the doors at the rear. At sight of RADOST, he immediately goes out through the other door, humming as he disappears. RADOST, rushing after him.)
Here, wait!
(Leading GUSTAVE by the arm.)
You cheeky sparrow! Caught you nicely!
(Looks him in the eye and pauses before speaking.)
What did "Forgive me, Uncle!" mean – precisely?

GUSTAVE: Just so –

RADOST: How so?

GUSTAVE: 'Twas so …

RADOST: I heard right?
"Just so" … ?

GUSTAVE: 'Twas nothing …

RADOST: Nothing?

GUSTAVE: No …

RADOST: I see …
"Forgive me, Uncle – pity on my plight …"?

GUSTAVE: Quite simple, for with love, as all agree,
It happens now and then – things go awry:
One quarrels, there's a tiff – and love may try,
Carried away by pure emotion's strength,
To fight against itself, may go the length …
But in the last resort, the game's played out!
There, Uncle … now you know what it's about!

164

GUSTAVE prepares to leave.

RADOST: *(Restraining him.)*
Hold hard! To me, that's anything but clear!

GUSTAVE: It's clear as I can make it, Uncle dear!

RADOST: Why were you kneeling then, as though in prayer?

GUSTAVE: *(Pretending to be indignant.)*
You don't believe me, Uncle? That's unfair!
(Makes as if to go.)
If that's the way of it, then I'll not stay.
I'll call a carriage and be on my way.
Jan! Hey, Jan!

RADOST: *(Goes after him, pats his shoulder.)*
How, now, Gustave! Don't take offence!

GUSTAVE: *(Pretending anger, walks on.)*
When I say something –

RADOST: Easy! Why so tense?

GUSTAVE: I've told you all – precise and clear as day!

RADOST: Of course, of course … Don't doubt a word you say!
(To himself.)
He's like saltpetre! Sparkle, flash and flame!

GUSTAVE: *(Hugging him.)*
My own dear uncle!

RADOST: Gustave, my dear boy!
(Mournfully.)
You scorn advice –

GUSTAVE: Not so – I always aim
To win your praise and to afford you joy.

RADOST: But why should Clara …

GUSTAVE: Clara, yet again!
God's punishment for me, the scourge of men!
She's everywhere … won't mind her own affairs,
Cocksure, pig-headed, certain she knows best –
For ever crowing!

(Demonstrating.)

                  Damn her stuck-up airs!
For universal concord, I'd suggest,
Dear Uncle –

RADOST: What?

GUSTAVE: You marry her …

RADOST: Insane!

GUSTAVE: Do me the favour!

RADOST: Just what I'd expect!

GUSTAVE: She plagues me!

RADOST: *(Shrugging.)*

                Therefore, some old man like me … ?
She'll cease to trouble you, if you'll refrain
From doing all you can, as I suspect,
To make Albin rebel.

GUSTAVE: Just what he's done!

RADOST: How so?

GUSTAVE: For him, Aniela is the one!

RADOST: For *him*?

GUSTAVE: The only one!

RADOST: That cannot be!

GUSTAVE: Head over heels in love! He's fit to die!
I'm serious, beshrew me if I lie!

RADOST: Albin!?

GUSTAVE: He's much too fly to show his hand!
Albin's a master of flirtation's art:
He woos the one, the other has his heart!

RADOST: But how are you and Aniela faring?

GUSTAVE: *(Long pause. He folds his arms.)*
What's magnetism?

RADOST: Eh?

GUSTAVE: You know … What is it?
Tell me …

RADOST: Can't see how that has a bearing …

GUSTAVE: They say that magnetism is a random force,
              Enabling life's vital flux to course
              Between two bodies. Given that I'm blest
              With power another's veins to fire with zest,
              Why should I not, to some young joyous heart –
              Pure as fresh-sprinkled snow – likewise impart
              The burning passion which I now reveal
              And, by sheer strength of will, the compact seal?

RADOST: Hanged if I understand a word you say!

GUSTAVE: I love and will be loved! It's clear as day!

RADOST: Clear, but too cocksure: the same old story –

GUSTAVE: Faint heart wins neither love nor glory …

RADOST: Loved you may be, but keep your wits about you!

GUSTAVE: Oh, Uncle dear! What would I do without you?

RADOST: What if I didn't think and rack my brains?

GUSTAVE: Uncle, I'm deeply grateful for your pains!

RADOST: Thank me if you see fit, but mend your ways!

GUSTAVE: I have! Uncle commands, Gustave obeys …
              I've every hope, all will be well with us
              If you'll just let things be and cease to fuss:
              In strife or concord, tumult or repose –
              Turn a deaf ear and let your eyelids close!

RADOST: What's going to happen?

GUSTAVE: Happen?
            (Embraces him.)
                             We'll be wed!
            (He runs off.)

RADOST: *(Following him.)*
            So little sense in such a swollen head!

END OF ACT THREE

ACT FOUR

SCENE ONE

GUSTAVE and JAN. GUSTAVE pacing to and fro, deep in thought, followed by JAN who holds a black handkerchief to be used as a bandage.

GUSTAVE: *(Holding out his left hand without pausing.)*
Bandage it quick!
(To himself.)
Yes, I'm in love! Deranged!
But she … ?

JAN: *(Following him, bandaging his hand.)*
It's nothing!

GUSTAVE: *(Stopping abruptly.)*
Nothing?

JAN: I can't find … !

GUSTAVE: My hand! Quick, tie it!
(To himself as he resumes pacing.)
Now, she's on my side –
But will she still be, once my role has changed?
How best to start?

JAN: *(Prevented from tying the bandage by GUSTAVE's gestures and movement.)*
Keep still, sir! Let me bind …

GUSTAVE jerks his hand away. JAN grabs hold of it and attempts to tie the bandage while walking.

GUSTAVE: *(To himself.)*
Bind – of course. We have a bond –

JAN: *(Letting go.)*
That's it!

GUSTAVE: *(To himself.)*
But how to loose it?

JAN: Pull the ends …

GUSTAVE: *(Stopping in anger.)*
                                 Nitwit!

JAN: Sir!

GUSTAVE: Fool!

JAN: Sir?

GUSTAVE: *(Throwing off the bandage.)*
                      Don't want the left one tied!
          The right hand writes …

JAN: But which one's hurting, pray?

GUSTAVE: What's that to you? Just tie the right one, Jan!
          (Holding out left hand, resumes pacing, while talking to himself.)
          First time I've loved …

JAN: But, sir …

GUSTAVE: Look lively, man!
                (To himself.)
          This love's quite different …

JAN: It's the same …

GUSTAVE: That's rot!

JAN: The left …

GUSTAVE: *(Holding out his right hand.)*
                      This hand, then! Haven't got all day!
          (GUSTAVE starts walking again, pulling JAN, who resists strongly. GUSTAVE still talking to himself.)
          I will be loved …
          (To JAN.)
                           You'll break it, like as not!

JAN: Which one, sir?

GUSTAVE: Let it be, Jan! Have a heart!

JAN: Bandaging's easy …

GUSTAVE: Silence is the art!

Enter ALBIN. At sign from GUSTAVE, JAN withdraws.

GUSTAVE: *(Aside.)*
The air grows moist ...   The fountain's on his way!
(To ALBIN.)
Unhappy Albin, as at break of day,
Your teardrops' dewy mist envelopes all ...

ALBIN: But can't erode the peak to'ards which I crawl!

GUSTAVE: If tempted nitric acid tears to shed –
Take my advice: try something else instead!

ALBIN: I need advice! But sounder than before!

GUSTAVE: Did I advise you ill?

ALBIN: For God to say!

GUSTAVE: What happened?

ALBIN: I was promptly shown the door!
Keep your advice on "how to rule" your way!

GUSTAVE: First let me cheer you ...

ALBIN: Me? I'm in despair.

GUSTAVE: But Clara loves you.

ALBIN: Joke in woeful taste ...

GUSTAVE: I vouch ...

ALBIN: I'll not believe ...

GUSTAVE: Then must I swear?

ALBIN: How could you know?

GUSTAVE: *(Pretending to take offence.)*
                          Then doubt me! What a waste!
Don't ask me to betray a confidence!

ALBIN: *(Hugging him.)*
Gustave, I'm lost for words ... my teardrops burn!

GUSTAVE: *(Patting him.)*
There, there ... poor Albin!

ALBIN: Loves me ... !?

GUSTAVE: She's obsessed!

ALBIN: What then?

GUSTAVE: We'll marry Albin, in a sense!

ALBIN: Me? Me? ... to Clara?

GUSTAVE: Yes, but ... in return,
Promise to play your part as I suggest!

ALBIN: Agreed! What must I do?

GUSTAVE: You know that oath
The girls have sworn, the source of all your woes?
Make Clara disavow it, pledge her troth!

ALBIN: Surfeit of joy!

GUSTAVE: You don't ask much, Lord knows!

ALBIN: Wed Clara! Heaven!

GUSTAVE: *(Aside.)*
                    Marry Albin! Hell!

ALBIN: Then what?

GUSTAVE: Listen!

ALBIN: All ears!

GUSTAVE: Make her believe
You love another ...

ALBIN: Quite beyond my power!

GUSTAVE: *(Persuasively.)*
Briefly ...

ALBIN: No, never!

GUSTAVE: A day ...

ALBIN: No, no!

GUSTAVE: An hour?

ALBIN: I'd sooner die!

GUSTAVE: *(Exasperated.)*
             Then die!

ALBIN: I can't deceive . ..

GUSTAVE: Don't! Just *pretend* your passion's on the wane!

ALBIN: I can't!

GUSTAVE: Make out your love has lost its strength …

ALBIN: Make out …

GUSTAVE: *(Pleadingly.)*

        Just hint …

ALBIN: I couldn't go that length …

GUSTAVE: *(Aside.)*

    Then go to hell!

    (To ALBIN.)

        Stay silent!

ALBIN: Until when?

GUSTAVE: One day …

ALBIN: Not speak?

GUSTAVE: Don't swoon!

ALBIN: All day?

GUSTAVE: Nor sigh!

ALBIN: Not even sigh?

    (Short pause.)

        That's hard!

GUSTAVE: *(Eagerly.)*

          For one day … Then,

The next, you can make up for it – you're free
To sigh and groan, to giggle, sniff and cry!
Meanwhile, from now on, you are not! Quite clear?

ALBIN: If one whole day, I honour your decree
And Clara notes I haven't shed a tear … ?

GUSTAVE: *(In exasperation.)*

Then, Albin, you'll be married very soon!

ALBIN: *(Brief pause.)*

Tomorrow?

GUSTAVE: If you don't speak or sigh or swoon!

ALBIN: Agreed …

GUSTAVE: You promise?

ALBIN: But I …

GUSTAVE: Do you?

ALBIN: Yes!

GUSTAVE: Then, off you go!
(Embracing him.)
                Best wishes …
(Turning him towards the door.)
                       Fare you well!
(Exit ALBIN.)
That'll keep Clara busy for a spell!
Love him or not, she'll find it very strange
That Albin's undergone so swift a change.
While she explores the mystery, poor soul,
I'll onwards, step by step, towards my goal!
(Enter ANIELA cautiously.)

ANIELA: Did Radost hear?

GUSTAVE: No …

ANIELA: Good! I'm so relieved!

GUSTAVE: No damage done …

ANIELA: I nearly died of fright …

GUSTAVE: *(Taking her hand.)*
Kindness so rare, I'd hardly have believed!
These many proofs of friendship's care excite
Within me gratitude immense …

ANIELA: What have I done such gratitude to gain?

GUSTAVE: You gladly do good deeds?

ANIELA: For preference …

GUSTAVE: Then you shall have your chance …

ANIELA: Do tell me when!

GUSTAVE: I've hurt my hand …

ANIELA: How badly?

GUSTAVE: Just a sprain …
The trouble is, I cannot hold a pen.
(Timidly.)

	Would you please write? Is that too much to ask?
ANIELA:	Write what?
GUSTAVE:	A note …
ANIELA:	I couldn't!
GUSTAVE:	Just a line …
ANIELA:	A line? To whom?
GUSTAVE:	To my Aniela, pray!
ANIELA:	I'm surely not best suited to that task?
GUSTAVE:	Why not?
ANIELA:	It's really no affair of mine!
GUSTAVE:	*(Plaintively.)*
	I've hurt my hand …
ANIELA:	Perhaps some friend outside … ?
GUSTAVE:	Grief so profound to whom should I betray?
	Whose services enlist? In whom confide,
	If my request to you should prove in vain?
ANIELA:	*(Takes a few steps, almost in tears.)*
	What shall I do?
	(Short pause.)
	No, no! I'd best refrain …
GUSTAVE:	Aniela, rich in all that youth deserves –
	The joys but not the sorrows of Creation.
	Still happy, still untried by separation,
	You can't know how the world's immense preserves,
	Can shrink at times to one concern abiding
	For lovers starved of some expected tiding!
	You don't know how the watchful eye grows bright,
	How breath is held at sound, however slight –
	The torment of hours lost to dalliance –
	With joys denied, long savoured in advance!
ANIELA:	If that's true love, love on against all odds!
GUSTAVE:	Love, yes, love! The rapture of the gods!

174

ANIELA:	But no!
GUSTAVE:	Why not?
ANIELA:	This love – I fear it still!
GUSTAVE:	Why fear?
AA;	I'm frightened –
GUSTAVE:	Only as a child

The doctor fears, who cures its mortal ill!
Nature by indifference is defiled
A soul, denied the right to love by choice,
No satisfaction knows in helping others,
Cold, calculation cannot hear the voice
Of tears, nor look on fellow-men as brothers!
It's when my heart with love is beating high
And I can say "I am in love" that I –
In sweet confusion, joyously aware –
Invite the whole wide world my bliss to share!

ANIELA:	How to be sure that true love can be found –
GUSTAVE:	There is but one love …
ANIELA:	Counterfeits are many!
GUSTAVE:	Why scorn a light with darkness all around?
ANIELA:	Love is so often false: why credit any?
GUSTAVE:	*(With feeling, holding her hand.)*

Don't trust the witness of my loving gaze,
When, as by chance, my eyes to yours I raise;
This trembling hand that now enfolds your own;
This voice that speaks with penetrating tone …
Let your own feelings rather be your guide –
Vague yearnings and desires unsatisfied:
The more so, since attraction, willed by fate,
Is but an echo of the other's state!
(ANIELA makes a gesture of disbelief.)
Some souls are born, believe me, to be mated –
Even if, sometimes, they are separated.

If not in this world, surely in some other,
They'll find, approach and join with one another –
As do the perfumes of two flowers, ascending,
Conjointly mingle, each with the other blending …
(ANIELA looks pensive, as GUSTAVE briefly pauses.)
Tell me, what do you think it was that spurred
Me on, to you alone to place my trust –
To you confiding all that we've discussed –
If not my heart, which never yet has erred?

ANIELA: But who then would abuse your confidence?

GUSTAVE: Clara for one …

ANIELA: Oh no! That makes no sense!

GUSTAVE: The more I'm hurt, the more she stands to gain.

ANIELA: Clara?

GUSTAVE: Whom Uncle Radost plans to wed!

ANIELA: Radost!?

GUSTAVE: Seeing his goal he can't attain,
He means to marry Clara in revenge –
Disown me – leaving all to her instead!

ANIELA: That cannot be!

GUSTAVE: It can! Radost won't change!

ANIELA: Clara'll refuse!

GUSTAVE: The motion's good as carried!

ANIELA: Her hate's sincere …

GUSTAVE: Sincere or insincere –
Radost is rich; her father is a miser.
As two and two make four, the picture's clear:
If not today, tomorrow they'll be married …

ANIELA: Her vows?

GUSTAVE: A dream! You'd really be much wiser
To quit that dreary path while time allows
And I'm still here, misgivings to arouse!
Is it not true, when thoughts in lofty flight,

Depict an image of extreme delight,
Precious, though trifling fancies often gleam
As brilliantly as flowers in a dream?
What is that radiance that floods the sight,
If it's not love, true love – steadfast and right –
Love that ensures the bridal pair don't falter,
As they take leave of parents at the altar?
Some say that *being* loved is joy supreme;
The joy of *loving*, greater still I deem: –
To make the fate of those you love on your own –
To live and feel on their behalf alone,
Your life for their sole benefit to lead,
Devoting every heart-beat to their need –
To make your world that tiny patch of sward
You cultivate – life's aims and life's reward!
Then, all vicissitudes being quietly past,
With hope to look beyond the grave at last.
Those are the merits of that happy state
Which you, alas, propose to abdicate!

ANIELA: *(In exultation.)*

Ah, never! No!

(Moderating transports.)

                I still can't quite decide!

(Renewed emotion.)

I'll write that letter, though! I would not see
A single tear-drop shed because of me!

(Dabbing her eye.)

In others' happiness, let mine reside …

GUSTAVE: You mean you'll write, you angel! You're so sweet!

You do so much … My gratitude's complete!

(Kisses her hand.)

If only you could read my innermost heart!

ANIELA: But Gustave …

GUSTAVE: Best not ask … I might impart

More than I should … more, even, than I need!
Paper and pen!
(Gazes at her entranced, holding her hand.)
In such a way?
(To CLARA.)
You'll understand, I know –
You sensed my plight … Forgiveness you'll bestow!
(Kisses her hand and leaves quickly.)

ANIELA: *(Alone, after a brief pause.)*
Hate them? Though girls may gossip, boast and prate,
It's not as easy as all *that* to hate!
From rage to hatres, true, the road's not long –
Especially after treachery or defection!
But if the hand she clasps has done no wrong,
How could a girl with hate repay affection?
(Enter CLARA.)

CLARA: And who was that?

ANIELA: What? Who … ?

CLARA: …Were you talking to?

ANIELA: Gustave dropped in –

CLARA: To dwell upon his woes?

ANIELA: Somewhat …

CLARA: You took your time, the pair of you …

ANIELA: We couldn't have been quicker, goodness knows!

CLARA: What news?

ANIELA: You won't believe it, but it seems –
The fact is – he wants to marry you!

CLARA: Me?
(Skips and claps her hands.)
Why, what a stroke of luck! Pure joy!
I'll roast and toast the rascal till he screams!
You'll have your fill of me, Gustave, my boy!

ANIELA: *(Peeved.)*
Not Gustave ... Radost!

CLARA: That old buffer dreams ... ?

ANIELA: *(Still irritated.)*
Radost! ... Not Gustave!

CLARA: Never!

ANIELA: I understand!

CLARA: I hate him!

ANIELA: Whether or not you hate the man –
Since Gustave will not countenance his plan –
He means to wed you ... purely out of spite ...

CLARA: And who, pray, would presume to force my hand?

ANIELA: Your father sets great store by gold ... *he* might!
Radost is wealthy, leads a rich man's life ...
'Twould suit them both if you were Radost's wife!

CLARA: *(Trying to conceal growing confusion.)*
I won't! I'm not afraid ... I'd sooner die!
Father may have a will ... but so have I!
I'm not afraid ... I'm not ...
(Suddenly bursting into tears.)
What shall I do?
If once my father has an end in view,
There'll be no stopping him! I'll be undone ...

ANIELA: For shame! ...

CLARA: *(Hits on an idea, after pause.)*
I know! Gustave and you must wed!

ANIELA: Wed? What of our vow?

CLARA: At least, let one
Observe it faithfully – me, if not you!

ANIELA: But Gustave loves another ...

CLARA: Then I dread ...
I must tell Aunty ...

ANIELA: *(Looking round uneasily.)*
It's a secret, mind! …
Go quickly!

CLARA: She'll advise me; she's too kind
To sentence me to death with that old bore!

ANIELA: *(Looking round.)*
Minutes are precious! Quick, go have your chat!

CLARA: Better the veil … or Albin, come to that!

Exit CLARA.

ANIELA: *(Calling after her in a low voice.)*
Clara! Oh, Clara … please … just one thing more;
Oh dear, she's gone … I felt it was only fair
To seek her thoughts on this bizarre affair
With Gustave … Never mind! I tried to get her,
Too bad she didn't hear! I'll write that letter …

Enter GUSTAVE, bringing pen, paper, inkwell.

GUSTAVE: Here's what we need. Let's start without delay!

ANIELA: I spoke with Clara …

GUSTAVE: *(Aside.)*
Fine!
(Aloud.)
But if she speaks …

ANIELA: Who to?   What for?

GUSTAVE: Well, Uncle … If it leaks …

ANIELA: I'll vouch for her …

GUSTAVE: What did she have to say?

ANIELA: Burst into tears …

GUSTAVE: I doubt she wept sincerely –
Whose fault but hers? Poor Albin loved her dearly!

ANIELA: And still he does …

GUSTAVE: He doesn't, I'll be bound!

ANIELA:	Of course he does!
GUSTAVE:	He loves … Not Clara, though!
ANIELA:	Who else?
GUSTAVE:	Why, that's his secret, clearly!
ANIELA:	What utter nonsense! Trust me, I would know!
	Albin's our neighbour; always been around –
	We know his every move and all his calls …
GUSTAVE:	*(Speaking reluctantly.)*
	Between the two of us and these four walls …
	Albin's in love, all right … in love with you!
ANIELA:	With me?
GUSTAVE:	Yes, you! His passion's plain to see!
	No doubt about it! He's in ecstasy!
ANIELA:	Good gracious! Why so suddenly, if true?
GUSTAVE:	He takes his time. After so many years
	Of such profound disdain as Albin knew,
	Could any flame still burn, so drenched in tears?
	Maybe propinquity itself endears:
	How could he live near you and not be captured –
	By goodness, grace and charm alone enraptured?
	You tell me …
ANIELA:	That's a funny thing to say!
	(Short silence.)
	So Albin loves me?
GUSTAVE:	*(Hastily.)*
	You take my advice:
	Don't trust him! Love that blooms in such a way –
	Inspired by spite – can vanish in a trice!
ANIELA:	Clara he swears he loves …
GUSTAVE:	He's half-bemused!
ANIELA:	He sighs …
GUSTAVE:	Politeness!
ANIELA:	Weeps!

GUSTAVE:	Just force of habit!
ANIELA:	But …
GUSTAVE:	Truly!
ANIELA:	*(Taking up pen.)* Then let's write!
GUSTAVE:	*(With emotion.)* Aniela, dear! *(Brief silence. ANIELA looks puzzled.)* Write … if you will …
ANIELA:	The name … I was confused … *(Writes, then – talking to herself.)* Me? In love with me?
GUSTAVE:	*(Jealously.)* That wailing rabbit! His cast-off love, his shabby switch appear To please you! Can it be, you're flattered?
ANIELA:	What have I done to merit such a question?
GUSTAVE:	Forgive me! It was fear … I erred. I'm shattered! The heart your heart desires, I realize; A heart that loves more than it dares confess, Though every word is fraught with love's suggestion.
ANIELA:	Let's write …
GUSTAVE:	Then write: "To aid us in distress, Heaven has sent an angel in disguise, Whose pen will bring our yearning some relief …"
ANIELA:	I hardly think that's something I can write …
GUSTAVE:	But I'm the one who's writing, don't you see? How else could I describe you and requite Your generosity beyond belief?
ANIELA:	Then let's get on …

GUSTAVE: Please write: "No need to worry,
                    The person whom my Uncle bade me wed,
                    Hates me …"

ANIELA: Ah, no, Gustave … not that … I'm sorry …

GUSTAVE: What shall I say?

ANIELA: Put something else instead!

GUSTAVE: You change it, then!

ANIELA: Oh, gladly – I shall hurry!

GUSTAVE: *(Reading over her shoulder.)*
                    "Now favours me …!
                    (Takes her hand.)
                                    She does?

ANIELA: *(Slowly withdrawing her hand.)*
                                    Must I declare?

GUSTAVE: Now that you know me better –

ANIELA: Yes …?

GUSTAVE: Maybe
                    One day we might be friends. Do you agree?

ANIELA: We are and will be …

GUSTAVE: *(With mounting excitement.)*
                                Always?

ANIELA: Yes, I swear!

GUSTAVE: An end to all duplicity and strife?
                    I love you, Aniela – more than life!

ANIELA: *(Starting back in surprise.)*
                    What's that?

GUSTAVE: *(Regaining control of himself.)*
                            Please carry on …

ANIELA: *(Bending over the letter, as though to remind herself.)*
                                    How did it go?
                    "I love …"

GUSTAVE: Remind me!

ANIELA: "love you more than life!"

183

What's next?

GUSTAVE: What next? Oh, would it might be so –

ANIELA: Then let's write on …

GUSTAVE: Your declamation erred …
The voice must free the thought within the word!
"I love" is man's great verbal indicator
Of duty to self, mankind and our Creator!
How could such words be ever spoken coldly?
You love your mother, brother, or a friend;
I … you; you … me. You must proclaim it boldly,
Letting your voice love's plenitude portend –
Look at me, please!

ANIELA: *(Looking at him.)*
I love …

GUSTAVE: More feeling … try!
(Instructing her.)
I love you!

ANIELA: *(Warmly.)*
Love you …

GUSTAVE: Still a trifle shy!

ANIELA: I love you … love you!

GUSTAVE: Good! Bravo! The fact is,
The better you declaim, the more you practise!

ANIELA: Write on?

GUSTAVE: Yes …

ANIELA: Someone's coming!
(Jumping up.)
I can tell!

GUSTAVE: *(Kisses her hand.)*
Till later, then!

GUSTAVE darts out.

ANIELA: *(Following him.)*
Your note!

(He's already gone and she returns with the letter.)
He writes so well!

Enter PANI DOBRUSKA.

ANIELA: *(Concealing the letter, aside.)*
Another's secret ... sacred trust!

DOBRUSKA: No, no!
Say what you like, you girls, but I shall go
And question Radost. That's the simplest way;
He will explain ...

ANIELA: But what of Gustave, pray?

DOBRUSKA: He's spinning yarns. That he's in love, I grant ...
But that Radost on purpose ... No, I can't
And won't believe he'd sanction such a ploy!
Gustave has faults, like any other boy,
He's young and handsome, though ...

ANIELA: *(Naively.)*
Why, yes ... that's right! ...

DOBRUSKA: One might become attached ...

ANIELA: Why, yes ... one might ...

DOBRUSKA: I know his heart is better than his brain ...

ANIELA: Far and away, Mama!

DOBRUSKA: He's caused some pain ...
Still, if you cared for him ... if he attracts ...
(ANIELA sighs.)
Radost blames shyness for the way he acts.

ANIELA: Gustave, just now, at Radost's feet was kneeling –

DOBRUSKA: True ...

ANIELA: And their words ...

DOBRUSKA: They quarrelled ...

ANIELA: With great feeling!

DOBRUSKA: But who'd expect it of a man so sage ... ?
For vengeance sake, to marry at his age!

ANIELA:	Darling Mama! Don't give him Clara's hand!
DOBRUSKA:	First, I must know what Clara's father planned.
	It's him I must advise and not his daughter.
ANIELA:	At least, Mama, let your advice support her!

Enter CLARA. As she and PANI DOBRUSKA start talking, ANIELA leave the room, surreptitiously removing the pen and inkwell.

CLARA:	I'm quite distraught. How can I seek redress?
DOBRUSKA:	Perhaps your father will be loath to press …
CLARA:	But what if he does, what then?
DOBRUSKA:	You must obey …
CLARA:	Some father!
DOBRUSKA:	Do not speak of him that way!
	Your happiness he seeks …
CLARA:	That's hard to see!
	Radost's too old!
DOBRUSKA:	But good …
CLARA:	No good to me!
DOBRUSKA:	Your father's will he may by right impose;
	All men aren't Albins – bear-led by the nose!
	Knowing your father, Clara, I would guess,
	That your comtempt for Albin he'd not bless!
	If this time, he allows you not to wed,
	Next time, you may have greater cause to dread!
CLARA:	But Radost's never seemed to need a wife …
	Albin's at least in love, shows signs of life.
	If I *must* marry … Albin might just do!

RADOST is heard clearing his throat outside the door.

DOBRUSKA:	That must be Radost now …
CLARA:	All set to woo!
DOBRUSKA:	*(Aside.)*
	If that's so, I had better not be here …

186

(To RADOST as he enters.)
I'll be back …
(Exit PANI DOBRUSKA.)

RADOST: *(Approaching CLARA.)*
I won't be bored, that's clear!
What are you pondering? Man's ruination?

CLARA: My mind is pondering on some information
I'd like to publicize … If I'm compelled
To wed a man by whom I am repelled,
He'll be the most impoverished on earth!

RADOST: Good Lord! What will occasion him such dearth?

CLARA: Nothing but parties, banquets, games and dancing…

RADOST: What's wrong with that? You'll have a lovely time!
I'm all for gaiety … it's life-enhancing.

CLARA: Parties I hate!

RADOST: Peace, too, can be sublime …

CLARA: I'll waste his fortune …

RADOST: You will need his clearance . . . .

CLARA: I'll seize my share to squander!

RADOST: Strength will tell!

CLARA: I'll cut a dash …

RADOST: One dresses for appearance …

CLARA: I hate display!

RADOST: Then, you'll save cash as well!

CLARA: *(Speaking swiftly and vehemently.)*
I'll cross him, thwart his every step and whim:
If he's *pro*, I'll be *contra* – me and him!
Chat while he slumbers, sob when he is glad,
Yawn when he's holding forth, sing when he's sad;
Scream when he reads and, if he's writing, jog!
An ill-assorted couple – cat and dog!
(Remembering something.)
If he's got gout, I'll trample on his toes!

187

RADOST: *(Withdrawing his foot.)*
Then I'd best keep my distance, I suppose!
I wonder, though, what sinner will be found
To wed you and do penance all his life –
Unless it be – as Gustave spread around –
My privilege to have you for a wife!
(Laughs.)

CLARA: Well, now you know!

RADOST: But I've no reason to fear …
Your words I doubt; I know your heart, my dear!
(Tries to take her hand; CLARA withdraws it.)

CLARA: I won't! What shall I do?
(Tearfully.)
I will not, sir!

RADOST: Don't be a baby!

CLARA: How I wish I were!

RADOST: Look at me!

CLARA: *(Turning away.)*
I know you!

RADOST: Here you see –
Your groom cavorting …
(Spinning round.)
At his wedding-feast!
(Laughs, adding seriously.)
Only a joke …

CLARA: Not funny in the least!

RADOST: Oh, please don't cry! No, that could never be!
As proof, I'll send you Albin – if he's there.
(Exit RADOST, laughing.)
Strange girl, indeed! A very droll affair!

CLARA: *(Alone.)*
Not jokes, but tears are what I see ahead:

There'll not be much to laugh at once I'm wed!
(Enter ANIELA looking pensive.)

ANIELA: Clara!

CLARA: *(After short pause.)*
                 Yes!

ANIELA: Do you know?

CLARA: What?

ANIELA: I declare,
            That girl that Gustave worships is thrice-blest!

CLARA: I've got no time for her! What do I care?
            Let her be happy if she will! I'm not impressed!

ANIELA: To be so deeply loved!

CLARA: *(Ironically.)*
                            As Gustave claims …

ANIELA: Why should he lie?

CLARA: His vanity's alarming!

ANIELA: He does know how to love … and he's so charming!

CLARA: Take my advice, ignore him and his aims!

ANIELA: You do not know that warm, enchanted feeling:
            To hear fond words pour forth from manly breast
            With soulful ardour – now, the ear they tickle,
            Course like a tremor, cheeks and eyelids prickle –
            From face to heart, those words – like tear-drops stealing…
            Then, from the heart – up, up and up they're pressed
            (Pointing to her bosom.)
            Till they enfold the throat with strangler's grip,
            And you – despite yourself – a sigh let slip!

CLARA: You're such a child! That's new to you, maybe –
            But I've got Albin … So it's not to me!

ANIELA: You did have!

CLARA: What?

ANIELA: Rejoice!

CLARA: Why?

ANIELA: He's converted!

CLARA: Albin?

ANIELA: Does not love –

CLARA: Me?

ANIELA: You.

CLARA: How d'you know?

ANIELA: Gustave told me …

CLARA: Albin's not deserted!

He sighs –

ANIELA: Politeness …

CLARA: Begs …

ANIELA: Just habit …

CLARA: *(Aside.)*

                              Can't believe her!

ANIELA: I'll go so far as to …

CLARA: *(Exasperated.)*

                    How far'll you go?

ANIELA: To say the burden, sadly, falls to me …

CLARA: You?

ANIELA: Me …

CLARA: In love with you?

ANIELA: He claims to be …

CLARA: So much for men! He blubbers like a beaver!
He pleads, he swears that love his health has wrecked –
And then, to cap it all, he dares defect!
All loving to forswear, how wise we were!
Agreed?

ANIELA: Let's find Mama and talk to her!

CLARA: Agreed?

ANIELA: *(Leaving the room)*

                The lunch is served. Quick, while it's hot!

CLARA: *(Alone, forces a laugh, then bursts out in a fury.)*

                Albin – that poisonous snake! He loves me not!

END OF ACT FOUR

ACT FIVE

SCENE ONE

RADOST and GUSTAVE.

RADOST: Gustave, my boy – confess – as God is good:
You're making mischief!

GUSTAVE: What? As if I would!
Uncle, I'm now in love – no longer crazed!
So sensible, in fact, I'm quite amazed!

RADOST: If only *I* could be – for half an hour!
Why is it, everybody looks so sour?
To start with, there's Dobruska; I agree,
She's vexed with *you*, you rake! But why with me?
At table there, we might have been thirteen,
So much ill-humour! Never like was seen!
Aniela trembling, pale, or cheeks ablaze –
Transfixed by her Mama's unwavering gaze;
Clara's laugh and chat, concealing wrath
Albin counting blossoms on the cloth;
You, ill at ease, bewildered and alone –
The only normal person there, indeed –
As much at home as Pilate in the Creed!

GUSTAVE: *(Softly.)*
Love, Uncle, love's the cause of all the bother …

RADOST: Aniela, Clara – yes; but not their mother!

GUSTAVE: A mother's not to love?

RADOST: You crazy loon!

GUSTAVE: *(Taking him aside.)*
Older the fiddle, they say, sweeter the tune!

RADOST: You're mischief-making! Feel it in my bones!

GUSTAVE: What an idea!

RADOST: Don't like those undertones!
                    I'll get Dobruska to elucidate!

GUSTAVE: *She* won't know …

RADOST: What?

GUSTAVE: … a thing.

RADOST: You addlepate!
                    Cajole, beg, curse – you go your own sweet way!
                    I'm wasting time! You heed no word I say!

                    (Exit RADOST by door right.)

GUSTAVE: *(Alone.)*
                    Dear Uncle, be assured joy lies ahead –
                    But I'll not spill my secrets out of season!
                    For once he falls in love, no chucklehead
                    Should choose, as confidant, a man of reason:
                    He listens to advice, applauds with zest –
                    But when he acts, he does what he thinks best!
                    (Enter ALBIN.)
                    Aren't I a good adviser – friend, what's more?

ALBIN: Yes, Gustave! Thank you for your sound advice!
                    Twelve times she looked my way, if she looked twice!

GUSTAVE: Sighed six times, no doubt?

ALBIN: Well no, just four!

GUSTAVE: For one who never sighs, that's quite a lot …

ALBIN: *(Sighing.)*
                    Her sighs are rare, it's true. We've all some vice …

GUSTAVE: Did you yourself sigh?

ALBIN: Once … but from a distance.
                    By accident – quite softly … I forgot!

GUSTAVE: When tempted, leave the room! Go for a trot!

ALBIN: Thank heaven for such valuable assistance!
                    What joy to have so wise a friend beside me –
                    Such good, sound counselling to guide me!

Embraces GUSTAVE.

GUSTAVE:	Just heed it!
ALBIN:	I'll obey you to the letter!
GUSTAVE:	Restrain yourself! If she should weep – just let her! Don't say a word!
ALBIN:	*(Pained voice.)* Although with tears besought?
GUSTAVE:	An "Oh" or "Ah" could bring our plans to nought!
ALBIN:	*(Heroically.)* You saw how I behaved at lunch just now? I suffered greatly; sweat poured from my brow! Each time she looked, I goggled at the ceiling – When she was unaware, quick glances stealing.
GUSTAVE:	That's the idea!
ALBIN:	She asked me for the water, I froze at once; then, salt and bread, I think – I didn't stir …
GUSTAVE:	You let her pour your wine …
ALBIN:	I did … *(Quietly.)* … then drank it …
GUSTAVE:	Good! … A man must drink! I wager you'll soon see a welcoming sign Of softening … Already, you have caught her Ogling you, observing, making eyes? Restrain yourself: that's how to win the prize! If she should offer all you've besought her, Trying with tender words, peace to restore – Just answer "yes" or "no" – and nothing more!
ALBIN:	Were I to perish, I'll do all you say! You've quite convinced me, it's the only way! I'll treasure this advice of yours like gold!

Embraces GUSTAVE.

GUSTAVE: *(Imitating RADOST's mournful tone.)*
Only, for pity's sake, do what you're told …
Don't lark about! Behave the way I do!

ALBIN: Gustave, I couldn't hope to equal you!

CLARA comes running in and catches sight of GUSTAVE, stops suddenly.

CLARA: Isn't Aniela here?

GUSTAVE: *(Looking round.)*
No sign of her!
(Aside to ALBIN.)
She says "Aniela" … but with you in mind!
Just you hold back …

ALBIN: That's always best, I find!

GUSTAVE: *(Aside to ALBIN, giving him instructions.)*
Sit in the corner! Don't make eyes! Don't stir!
I'll see to everything, rely on me!
(ALBIN sits in the background, out of earshot, while GUSTAVE talks to CLARA.)
Congratulations – yes?

CLARA: *(Ironically.)*
Undoubtedly!
What were you thinking of?

GUSTAVE: Your new intended!

CLARA: I know of none!

GUSTAVE: What? Aunty's not offended?

CLARA: *(Furious.)*
Master Gustave!

GUSTAVE: In a rage, I see!

CLARA: The joke's too painful!
(Begins to weep.)

GUSTAVE: Tears? Does that imply
That Aunty wouldn't relish the connection?

CLARA: Wed *him*? A hundred deaths I'd sooner die!

GUSTAVE:	In that case, things assume a fresh complexion …
CLARA:	How so?
GUSTAVE:	We're threatened by the self-same fate,
	So let's forget our quarrels, cease to spar –
	Instead join forces and – retaliate!
CLARA:	But how?
GUSTAVE:	How?
	(Long pause while he thinks.)
	I've not thought that far! …
CLARA:	Gustave, this is what I'd suggest you do:
	Pretend your Uncle's plan appeals to you
	And play for time …
GUSTAVE:	That's what I, too, thought best!
	Alas, Aniela with untimely zest,
	To her Mama the whole sad tale expounded:
	She was upset; my Uncle quite dumbfounded –
	Inquiries, questions, checks – by now, no doubt,
	The pair of them have had the matter out!
CLARA:	The die is cast! Oh, Gustave, can't we still
	Hit on some way to change things, if we hurry?
	If I'm importunate, don't take it ill;
	Time's short and Radost ravening to marry …
	Tell me … this girl you love … your troth is plighted?
GUSTAVE:	Be that as may be … here, I have been slighted!
CLARA:	Oh no!
GUSTAVE:	My Uncle's wish *I'd* gladly heed;
	Not so, Aniela –
CLARA:	She's your friend in need!
GUSTAVE:	She's very kind, no plea would she ignore;
	That merits gratitude – but scarcely more.
CLARA:	*(Impatiently.)*
	Can you not guess the rest?
GUSTAVE:	That I might well,

	Did I not all too clearly recollect
	A conversation in which you, mam'zelle,
	Destroyed the hopes which now you resurrect!
CLARA:	Let circumstance my turnabout explain!
GUSTAVE:	Miss Clara's changed, has she, with circumstances?
	But Aniela's under no such strain …
	What reason have I to suppose advances,
	Once repelled, may now elicit praise?
CLARA:	*(Impetuously.)*
	It's this Aniela, then …
GUSTAVE:	I want to wed …
CLARA:	To her alone …
GUSTAVE:	I would devote my days …
CLARA:	What's stopping you? Why don't you go ahead?
GUSTAVE:	Uncertainty …
CLARA:	That's past!
GUSTAVE:	She's mine … ?
CLARA:	By choice.
GUSTAVE:	Aniela, then – ?
CLARA:	*(Excitedly.)*
	She's spoken with my voice!
GUSTAVE:	*(Aside.)*
	That's all I need to know! Now that I'm sure,
	Do whatever you like; *my* goal's secure!
	(Turning round as he leaves the room.)
	Don't take offense that I should make so free:
	Time's short and Radost is a cunning man …
	(Emphatically.)
	There's someone who might yet forestall his plan,
	So tell me please, as briefly as may be:
	(Softly, pointing over his shoulder at ALBIN.)
	With him … Would marriage *totally* repel?

	You're silent … Need I guess … ? I wish you well, But Albin, you know …
CLARA:	*(With mounting impatience.)* I know …
GUSTAVE:	'Twould be one way …
CLARA:	I understand …
GUSTAVE:	Assure him …
CLARA:	What to say?
GUSTAVE:	Am I to leave … ? *(Brief pause.)* … with him?
CLARA:	*(Restraining herself.)* Who told you to?
GUSTAVE:	So I'm to stay?
CLARA:	What torture!
GUSTAVE:	Then, will you Take my advice?
CLARA:	Yes, yes!
GUSTAVE:	You've said it!
CLARA:	I promise solemnly …
GUSTAVE:	*(Changing tone.)* That's hard to credit! You swear an oath and call it sempiternal, Then switch, twixt dawn and dusk, from hate infernal To love! You savage me without remorse, And then, within an hour, my cause endorse! That's frivolous! Deny it if you can! Who would behave thus? Surely, not a man! Which, having said – with feeling frank and fervent – I'm honoured to remain your humble servant! *(Bows low and leaves the room.)*

CLARA: *(Brief pause.)*
          What is all this? The end of our campaign?
          He's playing tricks … Revenge!

ALBIN: *(Aside.)*
                              I must refrain …

CLARA: By trusting him, Aniela I've betrayed!

ALBIN: *(Aside.)*
          She weeps!

CLARA: I'm guilty, guilty – and afraid!

ALBIN: *(Aside.)*
          I've learned the art …

CLARA: Oh, I'm in agony!

ALBIN: *(Aside.)*
          Hell!

CLARA: Albin! They've avenged your misery!

ALBIN: *(Jumps up, but sits down again. Aside.)*
          I've learned the art!

CLARA: Have I no rights at all?
          Even to pity?

ALBIN: *(Leaping up.)*
                        Can't resist her call!
          (To CLARA.)
          You begged for pity. Has it been denied?

CLARA: How could you doubt it, knowing what they plan?

ALBIN: What?

CLARA: Radost … Radost wants me for his bride!

ALBIN: And you?

CLARA: I'd sooner die!

ALBIN: He thinks he can
          Compel you?

CLARA: It's my father's own decree!

ALBIN: *You* marry Radost? That, I'll not endure!
          One blow will both avenge and set you free!

Rushes out through centre door.

CLARA: *(Running after him.)*
No, Albin, stay!
(In the doorway.)
He'll murder him, for sure!

RADOST comes running in, followed by PANI DOBRUSKA, then ANIELA.

RADOST: Where is he? Where?

DOBRUSKA: Calm down, don't rant and rave!

ANIELA: *(Aside.)*
Stop him, Mama!

RADOST: You thought that I would plot … ?

DOBRUSKA: I couldn't credit …

RADOST: Guests would so behave!

DOBRUSKA: No real harm's been done …

RADOST: I think, a lot –
He's told you lies!

DOBRUSKA: Forgive him!

RADOST: Drat the youth!

ANIELA: *(Aside.)*
Mama, restrain him, do!

RADOST: *(Striding towards GUSTAVE's bedroom door.)*
I want the truth!

DOBRUSKA: Wait!

RADOST: Let me be!

ANIELA: *(Aside.)*
No!

RADOST: *(Shouting through the door.)*
Gustave! Come out here!
(Freeing himself from DOBRUSKA.)
Permit me.
(Goes to the door.)

ANIELA: Lord!

RADOST: I want this matter righted!

He's gone again!

(Peering through the keyhole.)

DOBRUSKA: If I might have your ear:

Let's quietly discuss the problem first.

RADOST: Why? No lack of proof! We know the worst!

DOBRUSKA: You're too excited …

RADOST: I am *not* excited!

ANIELA: *(Aside.)*

Don't trust him!

DOBRUSKA: This Aniela – who is she?

RADOST: I know of none – past, present, now or ever –

Save one …

DOBRUSKA: No doubt, her father you recall?

RADOST: I swear, in all my living days I've never

Known anyone whose daughter was so named!

DOBRUSKA: An age-old squabble? Bitter enmity?

RADOST: No squabble! … I've no enemies at all!

ANIELA: *(Aside to her mother.)*

He won't confess!

RADOST: That boy should be ashamed!

DOBRUSKA: You've not forgot the duel, I suppose?

RADOST: The du …

(Head in hands.)

What tales he's spun, God only knows!

DOBRUSKA: Keep calm!

RADOST: My dear good lady, I'm nonplussed!

I saw, I felt it – sixth sense gave me warning –

That Gustave had some mischief up his sleeve.

(Mournful tone.)

What pained me most of all, the cruellest thrust,

Was your refusal later to believe
I gave the boy what for – this very morning!
(Woefully.)
What more can I do? What else? … I know!
I'll warn him one last time against disaster!

Rushes out.

ANIELA:	Run after him, Mama! Don't let him go!
DOBRUSKA:	I'll run …
ANIELA:	Be quick!
DOBRUSKA:	*(Running.)*
	I can't run any faster!

SCENE TWO

ANIELA, with GUSTAVE in the background.

ANIELA:	*(Not aware of GUSTAVE.)*
	Radost's impulsive, but – at heart – a friend,
	Tears and pleas will move him in the end.
	He'll pardon Gustave, who will take his leave
	And I shall weep, but Gustave will not grieve –
	He'll just forget –
GUSTAVE:	I won't …
ANIELA:	Oh!
GUSTAVE:	That, I'll never!
	The links that bind us will endure forever …
ANIELA:	Escape!
GUSTAVE:	From?
ANIELA:	Radost – breathing threats and curses!
GUSTAVE:	I'll talk him round …
ANIELA:	Despite the grudge he nurses?
GUSTAVE:	He's fickle.

ANIELA: Is he?

GUSTAVE: *(Nodding.)*
                           Madly!

ANIELA: *(With a sigh.)*
                           Such a torrent! …

GUSTAVE: He frightened you?

ANIELA: *(Naively.)*
                           Why, yes!

GUSTAVE: Just bear in mind
              How deep your sorrow, were you now to find
              All changes cancelled by abrupt reverses –
              (Brief pause.)
              Including love, which once you thought abhorrent?
              (Another pause.)
              Your mother would agree with me, I'll warrant …

ANIELA: She loves me dearly!

GUSTAVE: Well, what happens next?

ANIELA: *(To herself.)*
              What do I say? Why ask me? I'm perplexed …

GUSTAVE: *(Taking her hand.)*
              Don't trust the witness of my longing gaze,
              When, as by chance my eyes to yours I raise,
              This trembling hand that now enfolds your own,
              This voice that speaks with penetrating tone:
              Instead, just let your heart dictate your course –
              True love alone stirs love of equal force!
              Your heart is dumb?

ANIELA: *(Looking him in the eye.)*
                           No …

GUSTAVE: *(Taking her in his arms.)*
                           Aniela!

ANIELA: Gustave, dear!
              (Breaking away from him.)

	That other girl … ?
GUSTAVE:	You were and are the only one!
ANIELA:	Your Aniela was myself?
GUSTAVE:	She was!
ANIELA:	You'd not deceive me?
GUSTAVE:	You need have no fear!

I did play false, though innocent, because
How else was your affection to be won –
When all attempts to woo you were frustrated
By prejudice, that kept us separated?

ANIELA: Then you were not in love? You haven't switched?
And I'm the one …

GUSTAVE: By whom Gustave's bewitched!

ANIELA: Then cousin Clara's …

GUSTAVE: From her sins absolved –
Albin loves her; she – him; that problem's solved!

Enter RADOST quickly, followed by PANI DOBRUSKA, both out of breath and unable to speak. After brief silence, GUSTAVE bursts out laughing.

RADOST: *(Turning to DOBRUSKA, standing behind him.)*
He's laughing!

DOBRUSKA: *(Mopping her brow.)*
So I see …

RADOST: *(Arms akimbo, to GUSTAVE.)*
A word with you!

GUSTAVE: Why not?

RADOST: *(Sounding defeated.)*
"Why not?" – what impudence!
Admit, my dire predictions made good sense!
You mischievous gossip! Now, no more ado!
This Aniela whom you love – how, when and where?

GUSTAVE: *(Taking ANIELA's hand.)*
She's here!

RADOST: Aaa – !

(Turning to DOBRUSKA.)

         Haa!

GUSTAVE: *(To ANIELA.)*

            Not so?

ANIELA: Why, yes!

RADOST: You see?

Who could make head or tail of this affair?

That duel you spoke of? Don't lie to me!

GUSTAVE: *(Taking him aside.)*

You know …

RADOST: *(Loudly.)*

           Where?

GUSTAVE: *(More loudly still.)*

             At a masked ball, was it not?

RADOST: Shush!

GUSTAVE: You happened …

RADOST: *(Trying to shut him up.)*

              Never heard such rot!

GUSTAVE: *(Shaking his head.)*

It seems …

RADOST: Speak softly …

GUSTAVE: *(Loudly.)*

          Well …

RADOST: You'll wake the dead!

Have you no sense?

Enter ALBIN, running, followed by CLARA. While RADOST is still trying to quieten GUSTAVE, ALBIN runs up to him and yells in his ear.

ALBIN: You'll not win Clara's hand

Unless you kill me first!

RADOST: *(Starting back in alarm.)*

          What's that he said?

CLARA:	*(Restraining ALBIN.)* Albin!
RADOST:	*(Rubbing his ear.)* Me marry Clara?
DOBRUSKA:	What's the matter?
RADOST:	A plague of lunacy! He's mad a hatter! *(To ALBIN.)* Who said so?
ALBIN:	You did!
RADOST:	Can't you understand A joke?
CLARA:	You asked Papa …
RADOST:	Who said so? Who?!
CLARA:	Gustave …
RADOST:	Gustave, your favours are unbounded!
GUSTAVE:	I meant to frighten her …
RADOST:	You did? Confound it! Am I a bogeyman to scare young maids? *(To ALBIN.)* And you, sir? Why so keen on notching blades? You love Aniela …
ALBIN:	Me? Who says I do?
RADOST:	Gustave …
CLARA:	Yes, Gustave …
GUSTAVE:	I'm an addlepate, Whose plots and plays have triumphed nonetheless,

Taking ANIELA's hand. They kneel together before PANI DOBRUSKA.

	Which now, Aniela, let us demonstrate …
DOBRUSKA:	*(She helps them to their feet, addressing GUSTAVE.)* I understand …
RADOST:	I'm lost, I must confess …

DOBRUSKA:	My daughter's hand to you I gladly cede!
GUSTAVE:	There's still another pair, let's not forget … Albin! Come here!
DOBRUSKA:	Clara, your heart is set?
GUSTAVE:	She's willing, I can vouch!
CLARA:	But …
GUSTAVE:	It's agreed.
CLARA:	If I could choose, I wouldn't … out of spite!
ALBIN:	But can't you?
CLARA:	No … I can't. I must! I must!
GUSTAVE:	Be joined by him whose honour tis, by right! *(Solemnly joins their hands.)* I wish you both the happiest of matches! *(Quietly to CLARA.)* So much for vows! *(Quietly to ALBIN.)* Albin, batten your hatches! *(Aloud.)* There! Now all's well!
RADOST:	Gustave, by all that's just, A word of explanation would be nice …
GUSTAVE:	*(Embracing him.)* Dear Uncle! Thank you – for superb advice!

THE END

THE ANNUITY
[DOZYWOCIE]

Characters

LEON BIRBANSKI
Young man-about-town

DOCTOR HUGO
Leon's doctor

ORGON
Gentleman-farmer

ROSE
Daughter of Orgon

WATKA
Money-lender, miser

TWARDOSZ
Businessman

RAPHAEL LAGENA
Friend of Birbanski

MICHAEL LAGENA
Raphael's brother

PHILIP
Birbanski's servant

INN-SERVANTS, MUSICIANS, PEDLARS, ETC.

The scene is set in a Polish city, in the early
nineteenth century. The play was first performed
in Lvov on 12 June 1835.

ACT ONE

SCENE ONE

The main hall of an inn. A door with a number on it. On the right-hand side, near a window, a small table on which candles are burning, glasses and cards, etc., are spread around. More of the same are littered on the floor, as well as a number of bottles. RAPHAEL and MICHAEL, asleep, are slumped on a sofa, left of stage. In the background, musicians with instruments in hand, are drowsing behind their music-stands on which are more bottles and guttering candles. Room in complete disorder, chairs overturned, etc. PHILIP tidying up. Enter WATKA.

WATKA: *(Peering in.)*
        Pst! Philip!

PHILIP: *(Snuffing out candles without looking round.)*
           Come on in! Why not?!

WATKA: *(Advances into the room, looking about him and shaking his head.)*
        Musicians! Drunkards everywhere!
        The room's a shambles! I despair!
        It's awful!

PHILIP: *(Yawning.)*
           Nothing wrong, I pray?

WATKA: *(Kicking a bottle.)*
        To judge the party by the wake –

PHILIP: They had a rare old time, I'd say!

WATKA: Night after night with scarce a break,
        Carousing, drinking, raising hell!
        No way to live! Their health will crack! –
        And Leon's anything but well!
        He can't take risks. These youngsters lack
        All sense! What can one do but grieve
        For youth that lives as though immortal?
        Tell 'em they'll die: they won't believe,

Till, blessed by priest at heaven's portal,
Or when they're lowered six foot under –
Then –

PHILIP: *(Interrupting.)*

They might –

WATKA: By then, no wonder!
Too late! By then, they've ruined those –

PHILIP: *(Interrupting sarcastically.)*

Who loved them best of all, God knows –

WATKA: Those who pay vast sums, like me,
In cash, regardless of the cost,
To purchase an annuity
Which, by tomorrow, may be lost!
It bothers Leon not a whit
That someone's paid to keep him fit!
His health's not *his* to dissipate!

PHILIP: *(Ironically.)*

True, once he's buried, it's too late:
Good-bye to the annuity!

WATKA: You're right! – then I'll be in a fix!
Broke in perpetuity!
I'm like a kitten on hot bricks –
Worried stiff – and I've to thank
This party at which –

PHILIP: What?

WATKA: They –

PHILIP: Drank!

WATKA: I guessed as much! Unhealthy! Foul!
But modestly? Or to excess?

PHILIP: Why, by the glass!

WATKA: You crafty owl!
Had you said "by the spoon", I'd guess
A hundred thousand spoons they sank!

	And what of Leon?
PHILIP:	Drank and drank –
WATKA:	Drank?
PHILIP:	Like a whale!
WATKA:	A whale! O Lord!
	The boy's his own worst enemy!
	Sparrow-chest and graveyard cough!
	As good as falling on a sword!
	Then they – ?
PHILIP:	Played cards, as you can see …
WATKA:	Played cards? That's something, I suppose:
	At least, my pawn-shop's better off:
	For losers who cannot afford
	To pay, get nothing for their stuff!
PHILIP:	I can't complain, myself, Lord knows!
	Ten ducats came my way last night –
WATKA:	Ten ducats, Philip! Quite a coup!
	Born with a caul! I envy you!
	You've started gambling? Well you might!
PHILIP:	Not I! No time for games of chance:
	I learnt my lesson in your school!
	Always be certain in advance
	You'll make a profit: that's my rule!
WATKA:	Ten ducats? Seems a lot to make!
PHILIP:	I sold new packs each time they played.
WATKA:	Sold packs of cards? Ten … quite a take!
	Uncommon profitable trade!
	I'd like to see those ten gold ducats –
PHILIP:	Nothing special – look, just ducats.
WATKA:	Not been clipped?
PHILIP:	Full weight …
WATKA:	Let's see –
PHILIP:	What do you mean?

WATKA: I thought you might –
Those ten … well … confidentially …
Man to man … one does what's right …
Hand in glove … I thought you might –

PHILIP: *(Keen to escape.)*
Can't stay!

WATKA: *(Holding him back.)*
                              You'd leave me out of pocket?

PHILIP: Rich Pan Watka, what's ten ducat?
Expect me to go fifty-fifty
With the profit that a thrifty
Servant makes from overtime
Night and day? Why, that's a crime!

WATKA: A crime it certainly is not!
One holds tight to all he's got –
The other tries to wrest it from him;
Fact is, Philip – I'll explain –
Just by going halves with me,
You'd reimburse my cash and pain.
When I bought that annuity
On Leon's life, I was concerned
A paragon of honesty
Should watch him when my back was turned,
To make sure that his precious health
Was guarded to forestall demise:
His life – which cost no little wealth –
Protected, cherished – like one's eyes!
And you I chose in recognition
Of your past record, loyalty shown
And for your steadfast sense of mission,
As overseer of goods in pawn.
Despite being put about no end –
The work involved and costs defrayed –
I got you taken on, my friend,

	Here, where you are amply paid!
PHILIP:	On which you charge me five per cent!
WATKA:	You should pay *ten* – the cash I spent!
	In any case, your income now
	Is thanks to me. You must allow
	I togged you out in lordly fashion!
PHILIP:	Togged me out? You cannot mean it!
WATKA:	A cap – complete with tassel, braid –
	A lovely cap!
PHILIP:	In shreds! You've seen it?
	Fit for a scare-crow, ready-made!
WATKA:	But what a tassel!
PHILIP:	*(Ironically.)* Lovely, splendid!
	What good's a gift like that to me?
WATKA:	It's got that tassel, don't you see?
PHILIP:	Confound the tassel! It's all frayed!
WATKA:	The lining's sound; not even mended!
	Two ells of cloth, on top of that –
	Gorgeous stuff –
PHILIP:	It's threadbare tat!
WATKA:	A sunshade –
PHILIP:	Very thing I need!
WATKA:	A pair of stylish boots –
PHILIP:	One only!
WATKA:	Made in Paris! Guaranteed!
	And then, that dressing-gown with flowers –
PHILIP:	Six years I worked for you, all hours
	And rich, indeed, my labour's fruit:
	A dressing-gown and *one* French boot!
WATKA:	We needn't dwell on that at present!
	When that annuity was bought –
PHILIP:	Bought? Extorted – more exact!
WATKA:	Come, Philip! No harsh words, my dear!

	You've got no call to be unpleasant:
	Extorted? Nothing of the sort:
	I paid out far too much, in fact!
PHILIP:	You very likely did, I fear –
	But why then write the title-deed
	In someone else's name? That's queer!
WATKA:	It's no concern of yours! Agreed?
PHILIP:	Why shouldn't Leon Birbanski learn
	What you conceal so avidly?
	Who owns the said annuity?
	Who is it pockets the return? –
	Afraid aspersions might be cast?
WATKA:	You're sprouting devil's antlers fast!
PHILIP:	Let them flourish as they will;
	They'll not prick you for very long:
	This wretched job's not worth a song.
	I'm leaving! Now Birbanski's ill,
	Find someone else to nurse him, pray!
WATKA:	What? Slightly ill? Or something chronic?
	I'll get a doctor right away!
PHILIP:	He'll not be cured by doctor's tonic!
WATKA:	What's he got, for heaven's sake?
PHILIP:	*(Indifferent.)*
	Oh, consumption –
WATKA:	Whom God loves!
PHILIP:	A vein in his chest will burst –
WATKA:	A vein?!
	Burst? In his chest?
PHILIP:	He'll groan with pain!
	And that's it …
WATKA:	Scuppered! God forbid!
PHILIP:	Must be handled with kid gloves!
WATKA:	I'll call the doctor, dare not wait!

My hour has come! O cruel fate!

WATKA exits.

PHILIP: *(Alone.)*
Skinflint! Miser! Villain! Knave!
Am I – your sentinel and slave –
Not to profit when I can?
You think I've got no conscience, eh?
High time that I pushed off, old man!
The wind's begun to shift, I'd say:
I own some trifles; cash put by –
And Leon Birbanski, kindly soul,
Soon, like a lemon, squeezed bone-dry,
Will need to tout a begging bowl!

Enter LEON. Obvious from his appearance that he has slept in his clothes. He coughs frequently.

LEON: Philip!

PHILIP: Sir!

LEON: *(Sits down, head in hands, talking to himself.)*
Lord! What a spree!
Capital in every way!
Pockets empty! Temples throb …
Philip!

PHILIP: Sir!

LEON: Soup?

PHILIP: Right away!

LEON: Sour, I hope?

PHILIP: Cook knows his job -
The finest *barshch* –

LEON: *(Calling after him.)*
And water, pray!
With sugar!

PHILIP:	*(Turning back.)*
	I shall see to it –
	And lemon, too? A teeny bit?
	Yes?
LEON:	Fine!
	(Calling after him.)
	No! That I detest –
	My head is splitting; tickly chest!
	I feel that feeble, I could faint –
	And you're suggesting lemonade!
	To hell with that advice – old maid!
PHILIP:	In that case, p'raps –
LEON:	For my complaint –
PHILIP:	A drop or two of –
LEON:	Yes? Of what?
PHILIP:	Of rum?
LEON:	Hmm … Wouldn't mind a tot!
	(Calling after him.)
	No water, though! I like it dry:
	The devil take soft drinks, say I!
	I'll do my health no good, it's true –
	I must be crazy to succumb!
	The fact is, if I must drink rum,
	I'd sooner not drink water, too.
	You might just fetch me half a bot.,
	Rosetree label, if you would …
	(Exit PHILIP. LEON continues after pause.)
	I always find rum does me good.
	(Pauses again, then approaches the two asleep.)
	Dear old Raphael! Good old Mike!
	Two brothers very much alike!
	What the devil? Raphael's bruised!
	A heavy card Jan must have used
	To raise that swelling on his pate!

Hope he'll believe us when we state
That he was dreaming all the while.
(Short silence.)
So far, I've lived it up in style:
Parties, card-games, banquets, balls –
But who's to say what next befalls?
I'm left with neither hut nor hovel –
Wardrobes empty, cupboards bare;
As for credit – vain to linger!
Good as done for – final grovel!
Scarce the strength to crook a finger!
(Short silence.)
What the deuce can I do now?
There's a thought! Might take a vow –
In some monastery repent,
Write my will and testament:
Eighteen hundred and thirty-five –
First year of my misfortune – I've
Bequeathed my –
(Bass-viol player, suddenly waking up, scrapes his bow once or twice.)
          Who's there? What's that noise?

PHILIP: *(Offstage.)*
           Coming, sir!
           (Enters.)
               It's only me.
           (Brings the rum.)

LEON: Throw out these fiddlers and their toys!
           All cards and bottles – out of sight!

PHILIP: Don't worry, I'll soon have them cleared!
           But, sir – you'll want to be polite –
           Our good friend has been waiting ages –

LEON: Who's that?

PHILIP: … With the short red beard!

LEON: No matter if his beard were blue,
        An empty purse can't pay what's due;
        You know –

PHILIP: The court has bade him call –
        A summons –
        (Gestures to indicate money.)

LEON: Box his ears – that's all!

PHILIP: But, sir, suppose he should return
        The compliment –

LEON: Then, you'll receive it!
        Our Jewish brethren must learn –
        Your job to see they all believe it –
        That, from today, I shall assist 'em
        With my new budgetary system,
        By which, I've reckoned, to a hair,
        What I have left or may possess –
        And not one penny can I spare.
        But, while we're talking about pelf,
        I told you to investigate –
        For I must know – I cannot wait –
        Where – in what cavern, swamp or hole –
        The cursed wretch has hid himself,
        Who snatched my pension, rot his soul!
        I want the rogue identified!
        I'll take the swindler aside
        And force him either to agree –
        To right the wrong he's done to me –
        Or else – I'll beat him black and blue!

PHILIP: Each option's better than the last:
        Three mortars deadlier than two.
        But all's in vain; the time is past:
        Berlin is where the rascal is:
        He draws your pension on due date
        Collecting it, as though twere his,

220

	Through bankers here, the reprobate!
	The man's still waiting, sir, to know –
LEON:	Tell him I'm furious; he'd best go!
PHILIP:	Won't listen –
LEON:	Won't he? Bend his ear!
PHILIP:	He says he will not budge from here!
LEON:	*(Striking table with his fist.)*
	He'll change his tune, if flung downstairs!
FIDDLER:	*(Suddenly waking up.)*
	A tune? At once …
	(To his fellow musicians.)
	Quick, tuneful airs!
	(All start playing false notes out of time.)
LEON:	For God's sake, quiet! Blast you, stop!
PHILIP:	*(Trying in vain to snatch their bows.)*
	Quiet! Enough! Get moving fast!
FIDDLER:	Can't help dozing … Fit to drop!
PHILIP:	*(Hustling them towards the door.)*
	Come on! Quick march!
FIDDLER:	*(In the doorway.)*
	A march, you'd like?
	At once, sir!
	(They strike up a march.)
PHILIP:	*(Shutting the door.)*
	Thank the Lord! At last!
	Some devil tuned their strings his way:
	They drink all night and *now* they play!

Music is heard fading away in distance. As PHILIP returns, an unseen clarinettist who's been lying in the corner, hidden by the music stands, strikes up false accompaniment. PHILIP walks towards him.

	Yet another! Damn and blast!!
CLARINETTIST:	My clarinet's a trifle dry!

PHILIP:	Sounds a trifle wet to me!
CLARINETTIST:	I must –
PHILIP:	*(Piloting him out the door.)*
	To bed! Sleep well!
	(Shutting the door behind him.)
	Good-bye!

Exit PHILIP after collecting candles.

SCENE TWO

LEON, RAPHAEL, MICHAEL.

RAPHAEL:	*(Having just woken up, lies there singing.)*
	When we get a chance to toast,
	Be it night or day –
	Drink a health unto our host,
	Provided he will pay!
MICHAEL:	*(Wakes up with a start, sits up.)*
	Where *are* we? Who's health is it?
	(Both, still sitting, gaze around them curiously. Short silence.)
LEON:	Good-day!
RAPHAEL:	It's Leon! Large as life!
	That was some party! But our visit …
	Word will spread all over town …
	But –
	(Starts searching for his shoe.)
MICHAEL:	*(With a sigh.)*
	A big "but"! Twon't be easy …
	This will take some living down.
RAPHAEL:	*(Still searching for shoe.)*
	I could have sworn I had a shoe!
	(Finds one, pulls it on.)
MICHAEL:	I've really done it, this time! Phew!

LEON:	What's the matter?
MICHAEL:	It's the wife!
	How'll I face her?
RAPHAEL:	Feeling queasy?
MICHAEL:	Worse than that!
LEON:	Why all this fuss?
	You fear your wife to that extent?
	She'll grouse and grumble; that's no joke –
	But she'll not send you up in smoke!
	Or cut your throat as punishment!
	There's really nothing to discuss!
RAPHAEL:	Easy to say! No doubt well meant –
	But someone's given me a poke:
	My forehead's burning: that's not right!
	(To LEON.)
	Inflamed, is it?
LEON:	A little spot …
RAPHAEL:	Mosquito surely …
LEON:	Earwig p'rhaps.
MICHAEL:	All said and done, a crowd of chaps,
	At such a party …
RAPHAEL:	Late at night …
MICHAEL:	It's going to cost me all I've got:
	Largely, Brother, thanks to you!
RAPHAEL:	Don't try to pin the blame on me!
	I'd just gone with a friend of mine
	To see my lawyer: I was due
	Back home in half an hour to dine!
	The meal was waiting … I'll get socks!
MICHAEL:	*I'd* gone out to book a box
	For "Norma", last night's opera –
	I've got the ticket here unused –
	When some ill-wind blew your my way:

"Come out with us!" First, I refused.
"Come on!" "Where?" "Herrings! Don't delay!"
Herrings I love; I couldn't wait! –
Those blasted herrings sealed my fate!

RAPHAEL: It seems to me, as in a dream,
That I played cards last night till broke …
You must remember that, at least?
(RAPHAEL pulls out his purse.)

MICHAEL: No …

RAPHAEL: *(Turns out his purse, then pockets.)*
See here, Brother! I've been fleeced!

LEON: Something's missing, it would seem?

RAPHAEL: Damn my eyes! It's not a joke!
Three hundred crowns my sister sent
To buy her this and that in town;
May lightning from the firmament
Blast country-dwellers and their shopping!
All gone! Most grievously I've blundered!

LEON: Tomorrow, you'll repay this stroke
By winning …

RAPHAEL: No, I won't! I'm stopping
No more gambling! Flush or broke!
Three hundred crowns! Oh God! Three hundred!

MICHAEL: *(Coming out of a reverie.)*
Just to help me to recall
What I was doing here at all,
Can *you* remember what took place?

RAPHAEL: I can't.

LEON: *(Laughing.)* All vanished! Not a trace!

MICHAEL: No laughing matter, let's be fair;
It might have been great fun, but then –
Raphael and I are married men!

LEON: No harm will come of it, I swear!

224

MICHAEL: An ill-timed outing, all the same! –

LEON: Don't worry, I'll take all the blame –
I'll tell your wives they needn't fuss …

RAPHAEL: That's fine! Then you'll come home with us?

LEON: I'll drop in later –

MICHAEL: That's no good!

RAPHAEL: Leon, I beg you, please consent:
Your gift for pretty phrases would
Defuse the sharpest argument –
Just drop my wife a line or two.

MICHAEL: And mine as well.

RAPHAEL: A note, a card!

MICHAEL: She really thinks the world of you.

RAPHAEL: Mine holds you in extreme regard.

LEON: Good, I shall write! I vouch that when
They read my notes they'll think no ill.
The trouble is that in my den –
There's lots of bottles but no quill!
A scorer's pencil must suffice –
    You'll have your letters in a trice!

Exit LEON. Brief silence.

MICHAEL: What will you say?

RAPHAEL: Me?

MICHAEL: What?

RAPHAEL: And you?

MICHAEL: Me? Nothing?

RAPHAEL: Nothing? Nor will I.

MICHAEL: But I can guess what I'll go through
The moment my good wife lets fly!

RAPHAEL: Mine won't utter, there and then;
With brow unclouded by displeasure,
She'll off to church and there at leisure,

Offer up her woes to God.
But just as soon as she gets back,
Her tongue will race to the attack;
Next day, she'll mention it again,
Alternate days; dates even, odd –
Later, weekly, then fortnightly –
Meekly, mildly and politely …
Like water dripping in a bath
Each drop of her relentless wrath
Upon the self-same spot descends,
Until, at last, the brain's drilled through!
Her chattering, nattering never ends;
She'd nag away till death was due,
Were I, at last, not so worn down –
As much for her sake as my own –
I swear all mischief to avoid,
Lest she have cause to be annoyed!

Enter LEON.

LEON:	Here are your certificates –
	Comprehensive, true, exact –
	Dead sober, eh? With forceful tact,
	I've sent them my profound regrets
	For keeping you two out all night.
RAPHAEL:	Ah, bless you! That should see us right!
MICHAEL:	In heaven, you'll be recompensed!
LEON:	I hope that, should they be incensed,
	Their anger will not long endure.
	Neither must know – of this make sure –
	The other's had a letter, too!
RAPHAEL:	Good, agreed: and thanks no end:
	You've helped two men in trouble, friend!
MICHAEL:	*(Kissing him on both cheeks.)*
	Would I might do the same for you,

Should God some day –
(With a sigh.)
                                   Grant you a wife!

LEON: Trust my defence to calm your strife;
               Don't ask me why! What's past, I fear,
               Is history – and no redress!

RAPHAEL: *(Taking MICHAEL's hand, puts on his hat with a
               flourish.)*
               Well! Best foot forward! Onward press!
               *(The hat is too big for him and slips down to his chin.
               Pulling it off.)*
               This hat –

MICHAEL: *(Trying it on.)*
                         Is not *your* hat, that's clear!
               Nor mine.

RAPHAEL: My head's not that inflated!

MICHAEL: *(Searching.)*
               But where is *mine*?

RAPHAEL: *(Searching.) Kind,* I call that!
               I'd barely had it renovated!

MICHAEL: I didn't *dream* I had a hat!

LEON: *(Pointing under the table with his foot.)*
               There's one down there –

MICHAEL: But mine was new!

LEON: I'd take what's left.

MICHAEL: *(Puts on hat which rests on the top of his head.)*
                              It nips my crown!

LEON: What harm is that? So did your own.

RAPHAEL: No hat? As well be headless, too!

LEON: Time's passing while you play the sage –
               Cover your pate! Should someone chide,
               Tell 'em your hat is all the rage!

RAPHAEL: Indeed … I like things cut and dried:

Wine or water, youth or age …
Courage, Brother! Let's advance!
What's done is done; we'll take our chance!

*Exeunt together, hand in hand, one wearing the hat that's
too big and the other the hat that's too small.*

LEON: *(Alone.)*
The curse of our society,
These married men who waver yet
Twixt marital propriety
And orgies of intemperance!
To teach them each the alphabet
Of pastimes innocent of blame –
From buying rounds to gambling-game –
Is torture, misery intense!
But when you finally succeed –
Nor is it all that rare, indeed –
The husbands put the rest to shame!

Enter PHILIP, carrying a package.

PHILIP: A parcel was delivered here
For you, sir, though it isn't clear
From whom or whence. It came today –
Apparently, some secret way.

LEON: You say a parcel came for me?
Light or heavy?

PHILIP: Awfully –

LEON: Heavy?

PHILIP: Light, sir.

LEON: *(Taking the parcel.)*
                Never mind;
Were it lighter still than dust,
The hand that brought it's gentle, kind –
O guardian angel, whom I trust –
You shelter me with loving wing,

228

And hover watchful overhead!
You are no unsubstantial thing:
Fresh proof of that each day I'm fed!
Perhaps the realm of Sylphs you share –
I dared to dub you my Sylphide –
My heart rejoicing in your care,
The focus of your constant heed –
But should you be of human race,
My mind's eye beauty so divine
Imagines, that my love's embrace
Awaits your soul, to make you mine!

PHILIP: What has this Sylphide sent our way?
You might just cast a weather-eye:
Cash wouldn't come amiss today –
You've need of some and so have I!

LEON: You're absolutely right! This day, I'm
Due to forfeit all I own;
(With emotion.)
Salvation in the nick of time –
A small advance, a bridging loan.
Or possibly, in far … Calcutta,
Some relative has ceased to utter –
An unknown cousin rich by right –
And Sylphide's sent a nimble sprite
With tidings of a legacy
Worth millions, all assigned to me!
(Lifting up the parcel.)
Whether dispatched from heaven or earth –
Bare now the secrets of your breast!
That I may calculate your worth,
For I am devilish hard-pressed!
(Unsealing the parcel, astonished.)
Ah!

PHILIP: *(As LEON extracts contents.)*

	A jacket and some stockings – two; A nightcap – though it's hardly new!
LEON:	*(Picks up the lot and throws it at PHILIP.)* Go to the devil!
PHILIP:	Not my fault! Sylphide should go, if anyone!
LEON:	Out of my sight, you useless dolt! Streuth! I'll teach you to make fun – I'll wring your neck until you croak!
PHILIP:	As if I'd dare play such a joke – *(Picking the clothes up off the floor.)* At least, it's flannel, nothing cheap – Warm and healthy – help you sleep.
LEON:	Shut up!
PHILIP:	Ha!
LEON:	What?
PHILIP:	A letter here … This nightcap, sir, could be enchanted; Perhaps the mystery will clear If, on your head, you'll let me plant it.
LEON:	*(Reading.)* "Respect for your health, at any cost, FOR IF YOU DIE, YOUR LIFE IS LOST."
PHILIP:	You see, sir? There, you see? You see!
LEON:	*(Looking around.)* No, I don't see – where's my stick? The whole thing strikes me as absurd …
PHILIP:	*(Retreating in haste.)* I'll go and check the anteroom.
LEON:	Wait!
PHILIP:	Just a moment, sir, I heard –

Exit PHILIP.

LEON: *(Alone.)*
The rascal's making fun of me!
(Short silence.)
And if it be as I suppose,
It's most insulting or plain dense
To send a pair of stocking hose
To one whose wealth was *once* immense!
(Short silence.)
Or, as I'd sooner far believe,
A friendly warning was the aim –
A curious method to conceive!
I can't be angry, all the same:
Whatever else, it demonstrates
That someone cares about my health –
That some untiring spirit waits
And watches over me by stealth.

PHILIP: *(Announcing.)*
Doctor Hugo!

Exit PHILIP.

DOCTOR: Sick indeed!
Leon's ill! Won't last much longer,
So I was told. At breakneck speed,
I hurry here, to find you stronger
Than all us medicos, bar none!

LEON: Ill? Who? Me?

DOCTOR: Had you not been,
Would I be here …

LEON: What can this mean?
Unheard of things are going on!

DOCTOR: How so? Was I not called by you?

LEON: Though always happy when you come,
Our old acquaintance to renew,
Forgive me, if I don't arrange

	To ail before – still less, succumb.
	Could you explain just why you're here?
	It seems a little strange!
DOCTOR:	I'd just left home, or very near,
	When someone, quite unknown to me –
	Out of breath and pale with fright –
	Unexpected – hove in sight:
	Fell upon me, clutched my knee –
	Begged me, pleading and imploring,
	In your name, for urgent aid:
	I complied – with utmost speed!
LEON:	That must have been my dear Sylphide!
	None but she could so persuade …
	Just describe her to me, Doctor:
	Beautiful? As goddess fair?
	Young, fresh, graceful – charms to spare?
	Tell me, quickly! Tell me, Doctor!
DOCTOR:	*(Laughing.)*
	Can't do that; I gave my word!
	Though it wouldn't have occurred
	To me to guess the name – Sylphide …
LEON:	That's the name I have bestowed
	Upon my guardian angel who,
	Hovering in my hour of need
	To shield me with a loving wing,
	Has so far never clearly showed
	Whether she's an earthly thing,
	Or else, some spirit interceding.
DOCTOR:	Heaven or earth? If you're in doubt,
	I see I've not been called in vain;
	What you need, my friend, is bleeding!
LEON:	Later – yes. First, hear me out:
	The past twelve months – well, give or take –
	A hidden monitor I sense

Who watches every move I make –
Precluding nasty accidents.
For instance, I am at a ball
Where violent squabbling begins;
At once, I'm shielded by a wall
Of dominoes and harlequins.
I visit someone and it rains –
I needn't say a word before
A coach is waiting at the door.
If something I've mislay or break –
Or, travelling, am lost and harassed,
Someone appears and takes great pains
To make sure I am not embarrassed.
And should I come home late at night,
A shade unsteady on my feet,
There'll be a lamp to light the street,
A helping hand to put me right.
(With a sigh.)
Thus far, my guardian with advice,
Rather than gifts, appears to bless,
But still, I'm grateful none the less:
Who's perfect? Save in paradise …

DOCTOR: All very odd, I won't deny …

LEON: So if *she* sent you, I'll admit:
I do feel seedy; throat is dry –
Head's on fire; I cough a bit.

DOCTOR: *(Feeling his pulse.)*
First, the head: you must be sure
A surgeon would advise you, brother:
Chop it off and fit another …

LEON: *(Hastily withdrawing his wrist.)*
Devil take you!

DOCTOR: Instant cure?
             Next, Sylphide …
             (LEON holds out his hand.)
                        Cough a bit?

LEON: I do …

DOCTOR: Eat enough for three?

LEON: For four!

DOCTOR: Twelve hours' sleep a day – or more?

LEON: Past two nights, not slept a wink …

DOCTOR: The cough, I s'pose?

LEON: No, cards … and drink …

DOCTOR: In layman's terms, the cure in vogue
          For gambling is a spell in jail!
          But Leon, joking quite apart –
          Unless you want your health to fail,
          You'll have to watch yourself, you rogue!
          She, whom you trust with all your heart
          To shield you, shelter and protect,
          Now warns you, with my voice and power,
          However briefly, to reflect
          That life grows shorter by the hour …

LEON: All doctors try to make one cower –

DOCTOR: Better a doctor's *coup de grace*
          Than ail as long as you exist!

LEON: I see you're a philanthropist!

DOCTOR: I'm talking to you as a friend:
          Ruin your health if, in the end,
          You're set upon an early grave.
          But even so, you cannot save
          Yourself, nor yet escape the mesh –
          The bitterness of deprivation,
          When, bereft of goods and cash,
          Penniless, the world you face.

You've grown too used to wealth and station,
Thinking as all gentry do,
That fear of ruin or disgrace
Need not dismay the likes of you!
Why stay alive if, through your fault –
A useless burden on us all –
You're forced to beg your bread and salt –
Day in, day out, compelled to crawl!

LEON: Sylphide?

DOCTOR: Fare you well!

LEON: Look here! –
My prescription?

DOCTOR: I shall give
To one whose penance, while you live,
Is looking after your well-being.

LEON: Why so?

DOCTOR: The wish was made quite clear
(Enter PHILIP.)
Your benefactor's keen on seeing
The chemist mixes, grain by grain,
What *you* may then pour down the drain!

LEON: *(Having read a note just handed to him by PHILIP.)*
Hurrah for commerce – and the sea!
Fresh oysters – just arrived, it says!

DOCTOR: *(Delighted.)*
Oysters!?

LEON: Come on, let's go see!
We can't let such a chance go by:
The first of them, you'll slit with me!

PHILIP: Oh, but – sir! Your health – it's plain …

DOCTOR: Oysters never hurt a fly!

PHILIP: Oysters, no – but with champagne!

DOCTOR: Just a glass –

LEON: Well, one or two …

DOCTOR: A couple, then –

LEON: *(Putting on his hat.)*
              A mere libation …

DOCTOR: Do no harm, with your disease.

LEON: We'll sink a few –

DOCTOR: In moderation …

LEON: I'm your patient, if you please!
              You lead the way and I will follow.
              (Taking him by the arm, propels him towards the door.)
              For quick relief, what must I swallow,
              Given my infirmities?

DOCTOR: What I prescribe will do the trick …

LEON: How well he knows what makes me tick!

END OF ACT ONE

ACT TWO

Music-stands and sofas have been put back in place; small table and chair, left of stage. ORGON, ROSE and SERVANTS. ORGON, dressed for a journey, wears a peaked cap. He has long moustaches, watch on a broad ribbon, etc. Behind him, Jewish pedlars and hotel servant.

SERVANT: *(Pointing to door on left.)*
Number Five: two rooms, quite nice –

ORGON: What's the daily rate in force?

SERVANT: We'll reckon up when you depart.

ORGON: Don't like the sound of that! The price –
I need to know before we start.

SERVANT: A dollar.

ORGON: Silver?

SERVANT: Yes, of course!

ORGON: A silver dollar? Devilish steep!

SERVANT: You'll not find anything that cheap!

ORGON: There's cheaper rooms all over town:
Why don't we make it half-a-crown?

ROSE: Don't haggle, Pa! It isn't done!

ORGON: That's stupid pride! I ask you, Rose!
He's not ashamed to try it on;
No shame on us, if we refuse
And tell him it's too dear. He knows
He's fleecing us. Why should we lose?!
(To SERVANT.)
Two paper dollars, then – a sin!
If not, we leave … Yes?

SERVANT: As you say …
For you – this once – so that you may
Have time to get to know our inn.

237

ORGON: *(To ROSE.)*
It does no harm to speak one's mind
That way, you've something left to spend!

SERVANT: I'll send your bags up –

ORGON: Very kind –
But tell me, if by chance you can,
How would I find the house, my friend,
In which Pan Watka lives?

SERVANT: The man
They call "youth's comforter"?

ORGON: His name
Is Prosper Watka, short and clear;
That's all I know. Must be the same.

SERVANT: He owns a tenement quite near –
No distance –

ORGON: Then inform him, please,
That here, Pan Orgon waits his call.
Matthew'll bring up our bags. That's all.

ORGON enters left-hand room.

ROSE: Were he just wicked, ugly, old –
I would willingly be wed
Since this sacrifice, I'm told
Is for Papa and family:
A money-lender, though, I dread –
Disreputable, crooked, cold –
The match would turn my soul to dust
And make a lunatic of me …
And yet – I must, I must, I must!

ORGON: *(Returning.)*
Such deceit you've never seen!
Two rooms, they say! It's barely one –
Divided by a simple screen!

FIRST JEW:	I'm an agent …
ORGON:	Thank you, no!
SECOND JEW:	Change your money?
ORGON:	Thank you, no!!
2ND SERVANT:	At your service!
ORGON:	Thank you, no!!!

How many more times? No, no, no!
Death and damnation! Go! Just go!
(They go.)
You've scarce arrived when, with a howl,
A mob of touts about you swarm –
Like jackdaws flocking round an owl!
*(PORTER arrives and gives him a handbill. ORGON stares
at him for a few moments; PORTER bows.)*
Take your tip! And don't come back,
My friend in splendid uniform,
Your kind of service, I don't lack!
(Exit PORTER. ORGON to himself.)
Let every servant serve who offers
And soon you'll find you've empty coffers!
(Reading the handbill.)
"The voyage of atmospheric exploration in a
gigantic balloon, which Count Karlo
Bombalini will shortly have the honour to
undertake, has never before been seen
in Europe. In addition, he is offering a free seat at
his side and invites any enthusiast
who may wish, to present himself at the above-
named location from which, at four
o'clock sharp, to the accompanying strains of a
military band, the balloon will be
released and rise aloft till lost to sight."
(Throws handbill on table right.)
May he be guided by the Lord –
Him, his balloon – free and all!

Whoever likes can climb aboard
And share this aerial odyssey –
Thanks be to God, it won't be me!
(MATTHEW, ORGON's servant, and DOORMAN carry in huge trunk. ORGON, repulsing the DOORMAN.)
What's this man doing with our kit?
Every minute brings fresh forces!
(To MATTHEW.)
Couldn't Mick take care of it,
Leaving Jack to mind the horses?

DOORMAN: I am –

ORGON: Just being kind, no doubt;
To hell with kindness! You intrude!
Kindness I hate, can do without –
Reward it with ingratitude …
(Under his breath.)
Or if need be, with my stick!
(To MATTHEW, helping him with the trunk.)
Be off with you, you oaf – and quick!
(They lift the trunk between them. ORGON, short of breath.)
Carries, tarries – uninvited –
Often enough –
(With gesture.)
            – he makes it pay!
Hovers till his tip is sighted –
Like a locust! Clear as day!

Enter WATKA.

WATKA: Your servant, sir – most dedicated!

ORGON: My dear good sir – you're well, I trust!

WATKA: Let me embrace you thrice – I must –
An honoured guest, so long awaited!
(They embrace. To ROSE.)
To you, my beautiful Miss Rose,

A hundred kisses I impart!
(Kissing her hand.)
Whether she's home, or travelling goes –
Her charms would capture any heart!
She looks as lovely as her name!
(Aside to ORGON.)
But why stay here, sir, all the same?
Did you just light on this by chance?
They'll pluck you as they would a linnet –
Overcharge you by the minute!
Mistake, not booking in advance!

ORGON: I know. We had no choice. A pity:
There's not a spare room in the city.

WATKA: I'll fix your bed and board tomorrow.

ORGON: I've no desire to linger here!

WATKA: What's wrong with Rose? A look of sorrow …

ORGON: Poor child!

WATKA: Why? You need have no fear:
I hope that she'll be far from poor,
The moment she becomes my wife!

ORGON: *(Sadly.)*
No doubt at all! It's just the lure
Of home and family and the past.
But I can promise that won't last.
She's a good child and she's no dunce!
Now, to save time, I think it best
If I go round the shops at once.
You lie down, Rose; take a rest;
Papa, himself, will buy your trousseau!

WATKA: Really, there's no need to do so:
Why, for form's sake, spend a ransom –
Helping Jewish business boom?
(Taking him aside.)
All you need of goods most handsome,

I can supply: from gems to loom,
Shoes, bedding – stuff for every room:
At pawn-shop prices, since it's you –
The tickets are long overdue!

ORGON: I don't want hand-me-downs for Rose!

WATKA: *(Aside.)*
Cross my heart and hope to die!
"I don't want hand-me-downs for Rose!"
What pride, oh, what enormous pride!
Hoity-toity! All a pose!
(To ORGON.)
Well, of course, 'twas just a thought –
Please yourself, what you decide.
(Aside.)
Let him buy new, then! Once he's bought –
And we are married, I'll arrange
Some to sell – the rest exchange!

ORGON: I must find out about my case.

WATKA: Afraid you'll lose? I hope it's solved!

ORGON: I'll tell you briefly what took place.
At last year's fair, I foolishly –
Impressed by urban chic – resolved
To have a tailor visit me.
The tailor came, equipped, alas –
With compasses and quizzing glass –
A ruler, sword-like, at his side.
At once, he spread the table wide;
And while I stood, amazed and tense,
The fellow took my measurements.
Twixt arms, extended at right-angles,
A vertical from my nose he drew,
Defined my paunch as three triangles
Added four more lines askew:
Below – two straight; then – crowning all –

Some semi-circles and a ball.
He then began to write, draw, figure –
Asked for more cloth to make it bigger,
And, having doubled his request –
Instead of a coat, he made a vest!
When I demanded recompense
A cobbler leapt to his defence;
Thanks to the cobbler's legal skill,
A year's gone by – I'm waiting still.
If, by today – the Lord forfend –
Proceedings fail to reach an end,
As sure as my name's Orgon, I'll
Dust that surveyor down in style!
So, for the nonce, I'll say goodbye –
Addy-es!

WATKA: Add-oo!

*(Both mispronounce "adieu". Exit ORGON. WATKA
continues, to ROSE.)*

          The promised day
For eager heart's too far away,
When lover is at liberty
On his beloved's cherished hand
To place a pure-gold wedding-band!

ROSE: *(Withdrawing her hand.)*
For me, that one ring will suffice …

WATKA: Pearls, gems, gold-setting – very nice!

ROSE: Gold, or silver – leaves me cold!

WATKA: But, Rose, my darling! Gold is gold!
Let's not talk poppycock, my dear:
We must be happy while we're here –
You take it! There, my turtle dovelet,
My little pigeon, cuckoo-lovelet,
Squirrelkin, my satin glovelet –
(Trying to put ring on her finger.)

Here, slip it on this slendereeny,
This one, here, this teeny-weeny,
Little finger –

ROSE: *(Wrenching her hand away.)*

No, no no!!

WATKA: Why, bless my soul! It's strange indeed:
I'm giving – yet, I'm forced to plead!
Unheard of! I don't understand …
Come, let me take your dainty hand
To show you love me …

ROSE: Love you? Me?
It seems you've somehow been misled!
I, at least, have never said it!

WATKA: Rose, you're blushing – to your credit:
It's of your own free will that we
Are very shortly to be wed.
(Rubbing his hands.)
Very soon now – any day
The capital will come my way,
(As though pointing to children.)
Then dividends will start to grow –
Just how many – who's to say?

ROSE: Yes, my own free will, I fear …
Papa – the facts are all too clear –
His debts to you could liquidate
Only by selling his estate …
Instead of that, he gave you Rose;
Which doesn't mean, as you suppose,
That I must love your honour now –
Or ever could discover how!
Wife I'll be – but just in name!

Exit ROSE.

WATKA: *(Alone, after short silence.)*
Six thousand rebate, all the same,
On what he owed: that's what she's cost –
Twas just the interest I'd made –
Still – high enough, the price I paid!
"Wife I'll be – but just in name!"
That's all I want – so nothing's lost:
Don't care if she is Rose or Violet –
Whether her gaze is warm or cold –
So long's she keeps my house inviolate,
Guards my caskets and my gold –
I shall have all that I require.
The problem's this annuity:
Must sell it soon or troubles dire
Will tax my ingenuity.
Birbanski's not a pretty sight!
Looks devilish ill, if you ask me! –
That graveyard bark by day and night –
That yellow face – he can't be right!
I'll drop from six per cent to three,
If Tvardosh offers cash in hand …
Why, here he comes! That's nicely planned!

Enter TVARDOSH.

TVARDOSH: *(Talks slowly, eyes constantly downcast and without the least change of facial expression. Aside.)*
Hasn't seen me … none the wiser;
Lost in prayer … Counfounded miser!
(Having approached.)
Forgive me!
(As if withdrawing.)

WATKA: *(Feigning surprise.)*
Dear old friend! What for?

TVARDOSH: Lost my way …

WATKA: Don't go. Please stay …

TVARDOSH:	They told me it was Number Four …
WATKA:	No, John, hold on! Don't run away!

(Putting an arm round his shoulders and gazing intently into his eyes.)

Best of luck and break a leg!
How very pleasant! What a treat!
You're wonderful to look upon –
(They shake hands several times.)
Younger, every time we meet!
Sit down – let's have a téte à téte …
(Taking TVARDOSH's hat as they both sit down.)
That's it … that's better!
(Laying hand on his knee.)

Dear old John!
(After short silence.)
And, now, what tidings to relate?

TVARDOSH sits up very straight, crossed feet hidden under his chair; eyes constantly lowered and fixed on his fidgety fingers. As though carved in stone.

TVARDOSH:	None.
WATKA:	*(After short silence.)*

Quite a wind today – bodes ill …

TVARDOSH:	*(After short silence.)*

Ill …

WATKA:	Why?
TVARDOSH:	The wind is blowing still.
WATKA:	*(Aside.)*

No talk of buying – yes or no:
He knows he has me – won't let go!
(Aloud.)
I can't help feeling quite depressed:
You never come to dine these days;
It's modest fare – you know my ways –
But company is of the best …

(Short silence – then aside.)
Like some damned brigand in his lair!

During the speech that follows, WATKA seems to be waiting for an answer after every time. But TVARDOSH shakes his head each time, as much as to say "enough of that". Aloud.

I saw today, you didn't buy …
Prices were better, by and by …
I didn't sell, though … must be fair …
I thought it kinder to delay …
Don't like to cause my friends distress
By profiting at their expense …

TVARDOSH: *(After short silence.)*
I thought twas far too much to pay.

WATKA: *(Jumps up, then sits down again.)*
"Too much to pay! Too much to pay!"
John, my dear fellow, have some sense!!
As well plunge knives of red-hot steel
Into my soul, as offer less …
"Too much to pay! Too much to pay!"
I must be mad! This can't be real!
Am I a Mason or free-thinker?
Am I a bankrupt? No, don't say it!
John, dear Johnny, do not say it –
It's really more than I can stand!

TVARDOSH: I don't say …

WATKA: Well, then – why not pay it?

TVARDOSH: Because Birbanski's ill … no cure …
He's bound to croak …

WATKA: *(As though thrown back in his chair.)*
Then may God's hand,
Shield his dear head, and health assure!
(With forced laugh.)
Never say die, John – stake my oath!;

Leon not well? That's nonsense pure!
Strong as Hercules! Mushroom growth!
Outlast Methusalah, for sure!
The way he's built! Why, what a frame!
His chest's enormous, head the same!
What bones! They're like a giant's, I swear;
You'll find none like them anywhere!
He's fighting fit, John, stake my oath!
Cross my heart and hope to die!
(Suddenly rising.)
I'd like a word, though, by the by –
One little word … and nothing more:
(Taking TVARDOSH's head in both hands.)
A hundred thousand, please –
(Kissing him on the forehead.)
                              – that's fair!
*(Springs back, looks around; TVARDOSH shakes his head
as a sign of refusal. WATKA darts forward and claps him
on the shoulder.)*
Ninety –
(Repeats performance as above.)
            Make it eighty then!
(Repeat performance.)
John, my dear fellow, valued friend!
You can't be serious! Heaven forfend!
Am I to be your sacrifice?
Don't squeeze me in a bloody vice!
(Grabbing hold of his coat and shaking him.)
Have pity, man! Some mercy show!
No conscience? No commiseration?
Sharp practice may work here below –
But spare a thought for your salvation!
Seventy, then!
(As above. TVARDOSH refuses.)
            It that's the way, sir,

Butchery is what you plot –
Better use a cut throat razor …
(Exposing his throat.)
Go on! Slice me – like a lamb!
Slay me quickly, on the spot!
I've lost my all! Destroyed I am!
Or beat my brains out! Set me free
From sempiternal misery!
(TVARDOSH tries to stand up but WATKA forces him down again.)
Make it sixty!
(Another refusal, as above.)
         I beseech,
John! May I lose the power of speech –
(Points to his throat.)
My leg be shattered into four,
Bones be stretched until they break,
If I should bate a shilling more,
Or half a shilling less should take –
Than – fifty thousand! …
(As TVARDOSH tries to stand up, WATKA pushes him back in his seat and says hastily.)
         Forty , then!
(Grabbing hold of his coat.)
What? Forty? Still the answer's "no"?
By the Maid of Seven Sorrows, deign
To pity me! You're merciless!
(Almost weeping with emotion.)
I'm poor, the victim of distress;
All but ruined, brought so low;
Naked I'll stand – sans home or fitments –
To penury by you consigned! …
And I've got family commitments!
Aged father, mother blind;
Upon my breast, they'll breathe their last …

	And soon I'll have a wife and children:

And soon I'll have a wife and children:
Pity, at least, my infant's plight!
Mercy on that blameless mite!
Johnny, for God's sake – life is sweet!
Don't put my family on the street!

TVARDOSH: *(Stand up and takes out his wallet – silence.)*
It's time I said a word myself:
(Silence – SERVANT enters bearing bottles of medicine.)
I'll not delay ... Look, here's the pelf ...
Take it or leave it ...

SERVANT: *(Standing behind WATKA.)*
       Please ...

WATKA: *(Impatiently.)*
       Yes, what?

SERVANT: For Pan Birbanski, are they not?
These medicines ... ?

WATKA: *(Grabbing the hand of TVARDOSH who's trying to put his purse back in his pocket, and shielding the SERVANT from sight – to TVARDOSH.)*
       How much? A lot?

SERVANT: Here, is it?

WATKA: *(Speaking directly into the SERVANT's ear.)*
       Get out!
(To TVARDOSH.)
       All depends ...

SERVANT puts down the bottles and goes. TVARDOSH picks up his hat.

TVARDOSH: Best cure the sick man first, methinks!
WATKA: Sick? Sick! He isn't sick at all!
You're quite mistaken, I'm afraid!
Excess of health is what they call
His problem. So, to slake his thirst –
To sap his strength – refreshing drinks

Is what the doctor recommends!
(Picks up bottle and drinks while speaking.)
Watch me! Look! It's lemonade!
Try a drop! Pure lemonade!
Taste for yourself! I'm drinking, see!
You know I'm healthy … fit's a flea!
Lovely! Capital! Look at me!

TVARDOSH: If you'll excuse me …
(Exit TVARDOSH.)

WATKA: Gypsy! Jew!
Turk! Renegade and parasite!
Could squeeze a farthing out of you!
(Shaking and spluttering.)
I'll light a candle when you croak –
Or promise one – since I'll be broke!

Enter LEON, slightly tipsy but not drunk, walks to the door of his room, humming to himself, but finding it locked, turns round and shouts. He coughs frequently.

LEON: Philip! Philip!

WATKA: *(Aside.)*
                              What a bellow!
He'll start that cough …

LEON: I'll shoot the bandit!
Philip! Philip!

Each time he shouts, WATKA trembles as though struck.

WATKA: Why is it you want this fellow?

LEON: What's that got –
(Cough.)

WATKA: – to do with me?
Nothing at all to do with me …
No need to tell me! I can guess:
I know the symptoms of distress …
I'd only ask you not to bellow!

LEON:	I *want* to bellow. –
WATKA:	Lord alive! –
	I say …
LEON:	*(Louder still. Following dialogue, up to the point that LEON starts coughing, is spoken very fast, almost simultaneously.)*
	Who wants to stop me shouting, singing?
WATKA:	Lord, O Lord!
LEON:	*(Close to WATKA's ear.)*
	If you don't cease …
WATKA:	*(Sotto voce.)*
	Your vein, your vein!
LEON:	What's that you say?
WATKA:	Your vein, your vein!
LEON:	My ears are ringing!
	(Starts coughing.)
WATKA:	St John deliver us, I pray!
LEON:	Go home and leave us all in peace!
	I *want* to shout!
WATKA:	*I* want to stay!
LEON:	While I've got breath, I'll have my way!
	Ha! hu! ha! hu!
	(Coughing.)
WATKA:	O Lord! O Lord!
	St John, the vein! Grant thy protection!
	Let me explain! You haven't heard
	The reason for my strong objection!
LEON:	I want to shout!
WATKA:	*(To himself.)*
	A waste of breath!
	(Running towards him.)
	St John deliver me from death!
	That vein! Deliver me from death!

LEON: Go to the devil!
(He sits down.)
                        Can one doubt
That Satan sent him? … Mustn't shout!
And yet I must … daren't put it off! –
It's killing me – this blasted cough!
(Buries his head in both hands.)

WATKA: *(Bringing a glass of water.)*
Sugared water, always best –
Take a sip; it helps *pro tem*
To irrigate a thirsty chest
And wash away that nasty phlegm …
I only mean to offer aid …

LEON: Then aid me!
(Drinks a little.)

WATKA: *(As though he himself were drinking.)*
                        How it soothes … refreshes!
Got to treat these bodies made
By God, much like our souls … They're precious!
Our flesh from harm He bade us save,
When He to man this body gave.
While healthily therein we dwell:
Life's a joy and all is well.

LEON: *(Nodding at the poster.)*
What's *that*?

WATKA: What?

LEON: *(Louder.)*
                        That …

WATKA: *(As though dealt a blow.)*
                        Don't talk, you're sick!

LEON: Let's see!

WATKA: Don't strain your chest. I'll check.

LEON: Give it me!

WATKA: *(Gives it to him.)*
                          Some lunatic
Is clearly out to break his neck –
Ballooning … Plans a record flight.
God grant his soul perpetual light!

LEON: *(Standing up.)*
Lunatic? Not so! Should we
Not rather envy him, aloft,
As towards the heavens' canopy
Of stars, in his balloon, he'll waft?
(As though to himself, ignoring WATKA.)
What ecstasy – albeit brief –
Amid the clouds, sublimely swaying –
Man's many follies, so much grief,
With sage's thoughtful eye surveying!
And as he rises, higher – higher,
This globe of mud, our world entire,
This ant-heap we inhabit – all –
Will paltry seem to him – so small!
And we, proud ants, who would walk tall –
Full of ambition, knowledge, pique –
Just comic creatures – puny, weak –
Who, with a spark of life begot,
Upon our planet's level face,
Struggle to rise above the mean,
As though the earth they walk had been
By bolts of lightning seared red-hot …
Each clambers on his neighbour's back,
Heedless who's trampled in the race –
Whose heart, or life's condemned to plummet –
That he may rise, enhance his stature,
And stand, one day, upon the summit! …
(Ironically.)
Of this world's mighty deeds, what trace?
That once were hailed supreme to nature?

The blood and tears of mass attack –
The cheers of murderers victorious?
What price here, what there seemed glorious?
Where are the voices then upraised
That Heaven might be duly praised?
High in the clouds, no sound – all's still;
The bliss of peace where none has trod!
Where one may breathe fresh air at will:
The further Man, the nearer God!

Falls to musing.

WATKA: *(Aside.)*
Quite delirious, I see …
Worse than ever … Lord, I fear
That vein of his is bound to shear –
Like weaver's thread too fiercely shuttled …
Once it does, all's up with me!
A cough, a rasp – his final gasp –
End of annuity! Watka scuttled!

LEON, lost in thought, and holding the poster in his right hand, approaches WATKA from behind and leans his elbow on WATKA's right shoulder. WATKA, under the weight, and after each movement backwards or forwards, stretches out his right leg. LEON looks straight ahead, as does WATKA. After a long silence, WATKA speaks in a low voice. Towards the end he sounds as though dolefully reciting a prayer.

Oh my God! he's all aquiver –
Trembling elbow, shaky leg …
Something frightful, lungs or liver –
What a weight! Good Lord, I beg!
His elbow's crippling my back!
Mercy, Lord! My spine'll crack!
I can't hold out! O blest St John,
Saint John of Kant and Simeon!
He's crushing me! God save my back!

I'm stuck! I've no way out at all!
If I move, he's bound to fall!
Lord! He'll break my neck, the wretch!
Saint John, Saint Anthony, I plead –
May God His hand towards me stretch,
Preserve me in my hour of need!

Before the last line, LEON holds the notice up and reads it.

LEON: Ah!

WATKA: *(Turning towards him.)*
                   A colic?
             *(Half seizing him, as LEON collapses on to him after
             disengaging his elbow.)*
                          End's in sight!

LEON: I see he's offering a flight:
             I'm his man!

WATKA: Catastrophe!

LEON: Within an hour – it's just past three –
             My head will cleave the clouds apart!
             Farewell to creditors! Let's start!
             Philip! My newest set of tails!
             Two packs of cards!

WATKA: *(Throws himself on LEON, grabbing hold of him.)*
                          No, no, no, no!!
             I won't permit this cruelty!
             I'd sooner die than let you go!

LEON: What now? Imagination fails!

WATKA: Don't move an inch!

LEON: Stand clear of me!

             *Gives WATKA such a push it sends him flying across the stage
             where, having pulled himself together, he begins speaking
             with a radiant, joyful look on his face as LEON, apparently
             quite fit, hurries out.*

WATKA: There goes my strength, my power, my cash!

Worth half a million! I could swoon!
How can I settle Satan's hash?
For he who falls from a balloon –
Is done for – sick or well – and soon!
(Searching for an idea.)
Burst the balloon? A trifle rash –
The owner'd kill me … Wait, let's see …
    I'll put him under lock and key!

LEON: *(Returning.)*
Philip! Where *is* the useless rake?
(Threatening.)
I'd give a lot to have him here!

WATKA: *(Creeping up on him.)*
My dear sir –
(Points at the left hand door.)

LEON: What?

WATKA: Hiding.

LEON: Why, for Heaven's sake?

WATKA: He's frightened.

LEON: *(Rushing into ORGON's room.)*
    Let me at the cur!
I'll show him what he's got to fear!

WATKA: *(Locking the door behind him.)*
Barred window; oak door – inches thick –
That should hold the lunatic!
(Places a chair outside the door and sits down.)
There you'll stay till four o'clock! …
(Jumping up.)
But Rose?
(Runs to the door – pauses.)
    Still – the annuity! …
My love … my thousands … woe is me!
All the same …
(Listens at the door.)

That's poppycock!
(Walking away.)
Trust to virtue, modesty –
Though modesty … Well, hard to gauge –
Certain it is, he's doomed to die
If once I let the rascal out;
If not, who knows what, in his rage
And fever, he may be about?
Protect us, all ye saints on high!

Enter PHILIP.

PHILIP: *(Aside.)*
Old skinflint's at his tricks, I see!
(Aloud.)
What is it, sir? Can't fit the key?

WATKA: Ah, Philip, there you are, my sweet!
I'm all in, barely on my feet …
Satan to our shores has brought
Some Count from Rome, in a balloon –
And Leon, by the fiend distraught –
Lord, pity us! – with this poltroon
Up to the stars is set to soar!

PHILIP: *(Ironically.)*
And human decency forbids?

WATKA: Forbids, indeed! And no mistake.
My precious capital's at stake …

PHILIP: And such a venture would deplore?

WATKA: *(Goes to the door, listens, comes back.)*
You've got to save both him and me!
Run for our lives! You get there first
And you can take the seat that's free!

PHILIP: *(Looks astonished, then smiles.)*
He'll call me out before we rise …

WATKA:	Play deaf!
PHILIP:	He'll signal …
WATKA:	Shut your eyes!
PHILIP:	He'll make a grab at me …
WATKA:	Won't reach –
	You'll be too high –
PHILIP:	Suppose he shoots? …
WATKA:	Bound to miss …
PHILIP:	No! I beseech!
	Don't like these upperclass pursuits!
WATKA:	But, Philip, you would never guess
	How lovely it will be up there …
	Ensconced upon a cloud … somewhere …
	Like Jupiter himself, no less!
PHILIP:	Praise me, praise me to the skies –
	Say what you like, I'll not agree;
	I may be simple, but too wise
	To let you make a fool of me!
WATKA:	You won't … ?
PHILIP:	I won't …
WATKA:	You're obstinate!
PHILIP:	That's true …
WATKA:	All right, let's say no more;
	I was just joking … Best forget.
	But Philip, listen – Pip, old son –
	Don't spare your legs, but quickly run
	To this balloon and watch it soar:
	Once it's up and safely so,
	Race back here and let me know!
	Look sharp about it! Don't delay!
	Seconds count! Be on your way!
	Philip, Phil, dear Pip – I pray!
	Quick as a flash and you will earn

A handsome tip …
(Puts hand in pocket, then hesitates.)
                    … on your return …
(Exit PHILIP.)
It worries me, there's not a sound –
No hammering at the door, I mean –
(Listens.)
Still as the grave … silence profound …
(Peers through keyhole.)
Can't see anything! Damn that screen!

Enter ORGON, two Jewish pedlars, with their goods, squabbling behind him. ORGON shuts the door on them.)

ORGON: What next? Won't let me out of sight!
These rogues are spoiling for a fight!

WATKA: *(Despairingly.)*
Orgon!

ORGON: Out you go!
(Approaching WATKA.)
                    Too steep!
The prices here are all sky-high …
Only our grain, it seems, is cheap!
Trust them to do us in the eye!
(Taking various samples from his pocket.)
There may be something Rose will fancy.
The names I've never heard before –
French they sound; my throat's quite soar:
Satin, I think, and sheveloo francy;
And this here's grogra – first-class stuff!
They say it's rare, but that's just guff!
Anything to fill the purse!

WATKA: *(Aside.)*
Speech or silence? Which is worse?

ORGON: She'll need a whole dress-length! Not too bad!
But women's fashions have gone mad!

Pleats everywhere – on top, below –
Pleats in front and pleats behind!
I tell you frankly I'd reject
A bride whose dress was so designed!
A man can't possibly inspect
In detail what the flounces cloak:
Girl in pleats? Pig in a poke!
(Exhibiting his samples.)
Advise me as a fellow male –
A pretty cover for the bed?
What's wrong? You've suddenly turned pale!

WATKA: Me? Pale? No … why?
(Aside.)
                    I shall drop dead!

ORGON: You're swaying …

WATKA: No, I'm just amused –
(Laughs.)

ORGON: A sure sign …

WATKA: *(Fearful.)*
                    … yes? What sort of sign?

ORGON: A sign your stomach feels ill-used:
Tartaric and vodka'll put you right;
I'll let you have some drops of mine.

WATKA: *(Barring his way to the room.)*
I'd tour the town, if I were you –

ORGON: But why?

WATKA: I'm just afraid you might …
Perhaps have only seen what's new,
Or just the older part maybe …
You ought …
(Aside.)
                    My mind is all at sea!

ORGON: Presently … *(He calls.)* … Rose!

WATKA: *(Silencing him.)*
                      For Heaven's sake!
         Rose can't hear! She's not awake!
         No good shouting –

ORGON: Don't restrain me!

WATKA: *(Beseechingly.)*
         Orgon, please, to see the sights!

ORGON: *(Gently repulsing him.)*
         No point trying to restrain me –
         Rose!

ROSE: *(From her room.)*
                 Yes?

ORGON: Come!

ROSE: I can't get out!

WATKA: *(Beseeching.)*
                      Orgon! Go and walk about!

ORGON moves towards the door, restrained by WATKA.

ORGON: Why *not*?

ROSE: They've locked me in too well!

LEON: And I'm cooped up with Rose, what's more –
         Like some Capuchin in his cell!

ORGON: What? Who? How?
         (Grabbing his stout stick.)
                      Who, in Heaven's name?
         I'll put a finish to his game!
         Open, or I'll smash the door!

WATKA: *(Dragging him away.)*
         Please, Orgon – go and see the sights!

ROSE: Papa, we haven't got the key!

LEON: A man called Watka, probably –

ORGON: *(To WATKA.)*
         The key! Or I'll give you what for!

WATKA: Please, Orgon, go and see the sights!

ORGON: The key, I tell you!

WATKA: Not with *me*!

ORGON: What the devil's going on?
Smash the door! I fear the worst!

WATKA: *(Stands in front of the door with arms outspread.)*
Stand back! You'll have to kill me first!

ORGON: *(To the centre door.)*
Who's out there? Come, lend a hand!

Enter a SERVANT and MATTEW, ORGON's manservant.

WATKA: *(Aside.)*
If Leon's hit, he won't survive –
At best, he's only half alive!

ORGON: *(To SERVANT.)*
Break down the door!

SERVANT: At your command!

WATKA: *(Arms outspread against the door, stamping and shouting at the top of his voice.)*
Violence! Vandals! Smashing, breaking!
It's my life, my life you're taking!
Sack and rape!

ORGON: His wits are gone!

LEON who, during the above lines, has been pounding the door so hard from the inside that he has also shaken WATKA, now bursts it open with a mighty heave, flinging WATKA into ORGON's arms.

WATKA: Hold him back! The slightest stroke … !
Hear me, all God-fearing folk –
Believe me, this is not a joke!
Keep them apart or I am lost!

ORGON: Leon!

LEON: *(To SERVANT and MATTHEW.)*
Clear off! Why, Orgon! Well … !

(Clapping him on the shoulder.)
Old friend! A lucky stroke of fate!
It's ages since our paths have crossed!
But I'm grief-stricken, truth to tell,
To find my Rose disconsolate –
My lovely Rose, beyond all praise –
My sweetheart since her cradle days –
My own dear mother's foster-child –
Condemned to wed a man reviled:
This Watka, with his crooked bill –
A miser's empty purse to fill!
One look's enough to realize
This owl-faced weakling, with cat's eyes
And falcon's beak instead of nose,
Is quite unworthy of my Rose!

ORGON: Leon, ah, my dear good boy!

LEON: Orgon, to see you, what a joy!
Words come easily to me,
But as for praise, I've got no call.

ORGON: Spare me a pointless homily!

LEON: You used to manage my estate,
And well you know it wasn't small –
But this you still don't know at all:
As from today, I've not a cent1

ORGON: But your annuity? …

LEON: It went …
Having confessed my sorry state –
There's something else! You know I love her:
Please may I wed your daughter Rose?

ORGON: Ah, Leon!

LEON: Do you not suppose
That I'm worth Watka three times over.

ORGON: But, Leon, this is lunacy!
She'll have no dowry – nought to share!

LEON: So? I've got nothing – nor has she:
               We're what you'd call a well-matched pair!
               (As to himself.)
               But Sylphide's worth a lot to me –
               At least a million!

WATKA: Can't you sell
               That property?

LEON: Not very well:
               More than half my life twould cost!

WATKA: *(Aside.)*
               Say half a year before its lost!

ORGON: For you, I'd lay my hand in fire –
               Yet cannot grant your heart's desire –
               Thereby, I'd suffer grief untold …
               (Exit ROSE, head bowed. ORGON continues with feeling.)
               Your wits, I always did admire;
               You've also got a heart of gold:
               To that kind heart I now appeal:
               Don't lead my pretty Rose astray –
               My sole support, my only stay!
               Consider her, consider me …

LEON: Wed such a man? This can't be real!

ORGON: Somehow, twill all work out, you'll see.

LEON: *(Turning away.)* Where's that balloon?

PHILIP: *(Rushing in.)*
                              Well on its way!

ORGON: *(To himself.)* Poor children!

WATKA: *(To himself.)*
                              It's my lucky day!

All stand in silent reflection.

END OF ACT TWO

ACT THREE

SCENE ONE

WATKA and TVARDOSH, seated at table right of stage. TVARDOSH facing away from the wall, counting banknotes. Two purses in front of him.

WATKA:	Oh, my God, how much I've lost!
TVARDOSH:	Oh, my God, what this has cost!
WATKA:	*(Handing him a pen.)*
	Sign it … sign it, John, m'dear!
TVARDOSH:	*(Laying out the notes.)*
	Two and three … makes five …
WATKA:	Sign here!
TVARDOSH:	Five, ten , five – than makes fifteen …
WATKA:	The ink is drying –
TVARDOSH:	Oh, indeed?
	Fifteen, four more – that's nineteen …
WATKA:	Why not do as we agreed …
	Just sign. I know I needn't fear
	You'll *cheat*! Between the likes of us,
	Confidence brooks no betrayal:
	We deal in thousands, never fuss –
	Hand in hand – cash on the nail!
TVARDOSH:	Two thousand, three – three thousand, four …
WATKA:	But Johnny, look – you don't suppose …
	A note in shreds I can't ignore!
TVARDOSH:	It's valid still –
WATKA:	It's lost its rose!
TVARDOSH:	Then it won't prick you.
WATKA:	Very funny!
	I don't mind jokes but I deplore
	Such humour when it comes to money:

	Too much at stake to play the wag:
	That fiver's like a cleaning rag!
	Come, Johnny, that's not fair, let's face it!
TVARDOSH:	I didn't issue it … can't replace it!
WATKA:	What the deuce? Well, never mind –
	We'll talk about it when you've signed.
	But, sign it now, John, don't delay –
	Sign, just sign, and no more chatter!
	Let's get it over right away!
TVARDOSH:	A signature's no laughing matter …
WATKA:	John, dear Johnny, for the sake
	Of God the Father, our true Lord,
	This painful quibbling forsake!
	Before you ever reach accord,
	You fuss and fiddle, bore and pester –
	Nag and niggle, play the jester,
	Till one's blood turns into bile!
TVARDOSH:	*(Coolly taking the pen.)*
	All my life, that's been my style.

Holding pen, looks around, begins to correct. Enter RAPHAEL and MICHAEL LAGENA, the PHILIP. TVARDOSH listens solemnly, pocketing the banknotes, packet by packet, while keeping his eye on the speakers.

RAPHAEL:	Where's Birbanski!
PHILIP:	*(Impatiently.)*
	He's not here!
	Again I say: he isn't here!
RAPHAEL:	Quiet, oaf!
PHILIP:	*(Cheekily.)* An oaf, sir? Who?
RAPHAEL:	Him I'll give a thrashing to
	If he can't hold his tongue! That clear?
	Look at him! Full of airs and graces!
	How he prances, boasts and prates,

	Stands behind a shabby chair – And on his spendthrift master waits, Who entertains without a care – Wasting cash he hasn't earned – While swarms of creditors are spurned!
PHILIP:	It's really not a servant's place To answer comments in such vein; The master'll soon be home again – No doubt he'll answer, face to face.
RAPHAEL:	Then let him answer – if he can!
WATKA:	Hush, Philip! Mustn't get annoyed …
RAPHAEL:	Today, this house shall be destroyed – This godless den of shame and vice … !
MICHAEL:	*(As though to himself.)* Where each man's virtue has its price.
RAPHAEL:	Today, let's sweep this threshold clear Of lewd debauch and scandal's sin – Where purses, tremulous with fear, At eve are fat, by morning thin.
MICHAEL:	*(Aside.)* Three hundred lost …
RAPHAEL:	This day of doom Will see the contents of this hell Sold to pay bills; the staff, with blows, Expelled; Birbanski in his tomb!

TVARDOSH stands up; WATKA looks terrified; exit PHILIP, shaking his fist.

MICHAEL:	My fury seeks revenge as well; For I've been hurt as much as you.
RAPHAEL:	Me first, you second, I propose –
MICHAEL:	Of course. I'm second, goodness knows! But one might also take the view, You went too far in what you said:

For where will all this squabbling get us?

RAPHAEL: *(Drawing pistols.)*
I'll shoot that demon in the head.
We'll bury him –
(Lays pistol on the table to his left.)

MICHAEL: If God'll let us …
But I'd remind you, if I might –
Though no one sure would deny
That Leon wronged us and should die –
He, too, has got an equal right
To fire a shot if there's a duel …

RAPHAEL: *(Offering his hand.)*
Then, let him fire but, should he kill,
You, Michael, will be living still:
You gave your word –

MICHAEL: And I'll stand by it …
But …

RAPHAEL: You agreed … You won't deny it?

MICHAEL: No, of course … but I confess …

RAPHAEL: This day, on earth, there'll be one less …
(Sits down at table on the left.)

WATKA: Cross my heart and hope to die,
If I don't know you both by sight!
Lagena brothers! Don't be nervous!
I'm … Peter Radost … at your service!
(He gives a false, noble-sounding, name, in an attempt to impress.)
My honour 'twas to know your father –
A privilege to know your father!
You gentlemen, too, I knew from birth –
Knew you as chubby urchins, rather –
Scarce knee-high above the earth –
Each as clever as the other:
Brains from father, looks from mother!

Since the family moved away,
There's been none like you to this day
In all the city, on my oath!
Cross my heart and hope to die,
If I don't recognize you both!

MICHAEL: I'm so delighted – joy untold –
To come across an unknown friend,
Must hug you! May I make so bold?
(Embraces him.)

WATKA: Your servant, sir, you may depend?
But, really, those harsh words of yours,
I was most deeply shocked to hear!
For fury such, what earthly cause
Could one so mild, a man so dear,
As our Birbanski, give? Explain!
My horror I can scarce contain.

RAPHAEL: What's there to say?

MICHAEL: He's used us ill!

WATKA: Come, gentlemen! "He's used us ill" –
For that, you'd murder him? You'd kill?
What grievous fault could that befit?
What crime could such a boy commit?
My friends, you do not realize –
Leon's an angel in disguise!

RAPHAEL: Not to a man who has a wife!
Devil incarnate – to the life!
A hare-brained, faithless malcontent!
He'll not escape our punishment!

WATKA: Although at times a bit unsteady –
Plays the jack-ass, likes a spree –
He's pure of heart – as pure can be!
As for his word, sound as the ready –
Solid as a title deed.
(With a glance at TVARDOSH.)

His business dealings dribble gold,
Though sometimes he may seem in need –
Once start, and he who would invest
Can count on profiting two-fold:
His interest doubling at will!
My good sirs, you're not raging still?

MICHAEL: Who's talking about interest?

WATKA: Then, had you capital at stake?

MICHAEL: Our capital is this affair –
He has purloined, the vicious rake!
And once our interest I declare,
His villainy you'll understand.
I and my brother chanced to land
Here briefly … in this house … last night.
And, though we wanted to depart, he
Made us stay and join the party …
Morning came and blows were struck –
Raphael's head got in the way.
Leon laughed at our ill-luck
But said he'd help to put things right
With both our wives – for, as you know,
It's different with a wife in tow:
Home on time or hell to pay!
So he wrote two letters for us.
Somehow, these were interchanged:
Instead of soothing, as arranged,
About our heads, a thunderous chorus –
All connubial joys denied:
Squabbles, jealousy, dissent –
Shameless, futile argument!
Once the floodgates opened wide,
It emerged, I'd have you know,
That Leon, just a year ago …
(Whispers in WATKA's ear.)

WATKA:	You're not the first or last, 'twould seem …
MICHAEL:	My brother, too … It's clear, the rat …
WATKA:	It smacks a bit of self-esteem To shed a fellow's blood for that …
MICHAEL:	Hang self-esteem! … My wife, my sweet!
WATKA:	Vain is this world in which we dwell …
RAPHAEL:	And you're a fool, sir – go to hell!
WATKA:	Cross my heart and hope to die! What a wit, sir! "Go to hell, Go to hell!" *(Embracing him.)* Why, you're such a treat! But, gentlemen, all jokes aside – Calm down, I beg! The life of man Is no mere trifle! Once you've killed, You can't pour back the blood you've spilled! It's horrible to think upon! Blood may flow – farewell to foe: But, later on … but later on! …
MICHAEL:	Brother, what a dreadful thought!
WATKA:	The celebrated Ludmir fought A duel in which he slew his friend; Thenceforth, his joys were at an end. No sleep at night; no peace of mind – And when, exhausted, he reclined, Then bloody corpses, one by one, Began to torture him for fun: They choked and tickled him by rote, Thrusting shin-bones down his throat!

RAPHAEL sit musing, MICHAEL standing beside him.

MICHAEL:	Brother, what a frightful thought!
WATKA:	I'll kneel to you, if that's your will – I'll even kiss your feet to plead!

272

(Kneeling down.)
There, I've knelt; you've got me – caught!
Forgo, forgo this loathsome deed!
Blood's appalling – blood you spill!

RAPHAEL: What causes you so much alarm?

WATKA: *(With increasing emotion, shared by MICHAEL.)*
He is my prince, my golden charm!
I reared that boy from infancy,
Caressed him, jounced him on my knee –
I love him as I would a son –
He's my delight, my only one!
In this wide world, he's all I've got!
If blood you thirst for, then why not
Take vengeance for a lapse so fickle
By shooting me! And may the ball
Strike here … My calf's begun to tickle!

RAPHAEL: *(Picking up his pistol and rising to his feet.)*
So be it!
(WATKA jumps up and shelters behind MICHAEL.)
          Michael, time we went.
His loyalty's moved me, after all:
Let's just forget the whole affair!

WATKA: *(Recovering his nerve.)*
That's wonderful! Magnificent!

RAPHAEL: *(Placing a hand on WATKA's shoulder.)*
There stands a man of virtue rare!
Could any foe of humankind
Reflect what such a heart is worth
And still, in honesty contend,
That friendship can't be found on earth!

Embraces WATKA and leaves.

MICHAEL: *(Kissing WATKA.)*
God keep you – and your cause defend!

WATKA: *(Seeing them out.)*
My gratitude you'll always find:
Some day this debt I shall repay –
Your servant, footstool and your slave!
(Returning.)
Cowards! Weaklings! Paltry fry –
Quick to threaten, shout and rave –
Face them boldly, and then fly!
Let's settle up …

TVARDOSH: They won't return?

WATKA: Won't stop till they're home and dry!
(TVARDOSH taking out the money.)
Sign! Just sign! Then you can count!

TVARDOSH: *(As to himself.)*
"I'll shoot and bury him," he said.

WATKA: Half gold, half notes – the full amount!

TVARDOSH: When one's thoughts have been disturbed
It takes some time to clear the head.

Enter DOCTOR.

DOCTOR: *(To WATKA.)*
So, you're the mystery patroness –
(Laughing.)
His "Sylphide" – with her matchless grace,
Her youth, her beauty, angel-face!
What is it this time? Shall I guess?
To help our favourite protégé,
You've something further to propose?
But pray don't cast that veil away
Which has concealed you for so long;
Far wiser to maintain your pose,
With wits alert should things go wrong.
My compliments on how you've trod
The thorny path of loving care;

However grave the sins you may
Have blundered into here and there,
The thorns will save your soul for God –
And earn eternal bliss one day!
Joking apart, before I go,
As a doctor, I must tell –

WATKA: Not now!

DOCTOR: He really isn't well …
Give urgent thought – you mustn't wait –
To Leon's health. He's devilish low …

WATKA: No! God forbid!

DOCTOR: In parlous state …
As well I know, since I've been, too …

WATKA: Dear Lord!

DOCTOR: The only hope of cure
Is to take all precautions due –
Else the disease will spread for sure.
Regarding your today's request …

WATKA: But …

DOCTOR: He was much as you described:
Yes, very far from at his best!

WATKA: You'll ruin me! …

DOCTOR: So I prescribed …

WATKA: No more!

DOCTOR: Sir! You must hear the rest!
Precisely since he's in your care,
My doctor's duty is to state
What's what, this instant – not too late!

WATKA: Ah! *(Horrified gasp.)*

DOCTOR: Don't be misled; his looks are fair
But Leon's ill – he's very sick!

WATKA: You'll ruin me!

DOCTOR: I tell you, if

He goes on living as today –
Continues drinking in this way –
Up every night and never sleeping –
No doctor's care will do the trick:
He'll not be long in our safe keeping!

WATKA: Doctor!

DOCTOR: I speak as one who shares
The grief which now afflicts your heart,
Consumption though, no victim spares:
And soon the moment comes to part.
Once spurred to action, in its rage,
It gallops on, from stage to stage.

WATKA: Woe!

DOCTOR: Scarce time to bat an eye;
It snuffs you, like a day-old chick!

WATKA: Oh, doctor! If he's bound to die,
To hell with all your rhetoric!

*TVARDOSH, throughout the preceding scene, has been putting
away more of his cash with every piece of bad news. He now
slips out unseen.*

DOCTOR: You'd best control this wild despair:
There's no alternative – so there!
It's up to him, his life to save:
Change his ways – or face the grave!

Exit DOCTOR.

WATKA: *(Turning, as though to face TVARDOSH.)*
Don't believe him!
(Consternation.) Gone? Then hell
Has sentenced *me* to death as well!
Into that wizard's swampy maze
Did I today, unwitting, stray?
Three hours, his gold has held my gaze
And now he's taken it away!

276

If from his throat I have to tear it,
I'll find who played me false, I swear it!
But damn by whom, or what was told:
The gold is what I want! The gold!
(As he rushes out, he meets ORGON with ROSE in the doorway; grabs ORGON's lapels in passing and shouts.)
The truth! Did you?

Hardly pausing, WATKA dashes out, leaving ROSE and ORGON, who is weighed down with parcels.

ORGON: Can't even stop!
Stung by a wasp and mad with pain?
The fellow's spinning like a top!
Has something set him off again,
Careering out and fit to drop,
Half-crazed, at risk to life and limb –
Moved by tender-hearted whim,
To double-lock some maiden's door?
(Ironically.)
Could one devise a measure more
Swift and effective? I admit
I've never seen the like of it!
Man lives and learns, the saying goes –
Until at last his eyelids close.
Come Rose, collect your bits and pieces!
(Depositing packages on the table.)
Crying again?

ROSE: You needn't fear ...
I know this Watka's rich as Croesus ...

ORGON: But when I see you weep, my dear,
I feel as though my heart could break ...
(Sadly.)
Leon misled you. Drat the lad!

ROSE: Not so, Papa – he made me sad:
Convinced me more than I'd surmised,

How much this Watka is despised
By everyone. Yet, him I'll take
To be my husband, share his name –
I'll even share contempt with him!
(With emotion.)
Perhaps the years my heart may tame –
Too virtuous till now, too prim! …

ORGON: You fear the whole world will despise you?
As to that, let me advise you:
Wealth's all you need, my darling, and
You'll have them eating from your hand!
Krentarski, my neighbour, and myself
Exemplify the power of pelf.
Though my moustache is rather fine,
My cap's old-fashioned in design,
I'm frugal, not much to my name,
Can't parlay French, I'll not dispute
For all that, I'd make bold to claim,
I'm still a man of good repute.
Yes, soon's I show my face in town
All round me people start to hoot:
"Squire!" they cry, and "Country gent!"
"Farmer Giles!" … and things like that …
Not that I let it get me down.
Still, parrot-cries and merriment
Are not so easy to laugh off:
I hear, I feel the people scoff …
Krentarski, though a thorough rogue,
Whose wallet jingles as he wanders
With cash extorted, which he squanders,
By fun and flattery stays in vogue;
As from a sling, he fires his lies;
He's à la mode, and dressed to please!
Day and night, *bonjour* he cries;
At cards, there's none will higher go:

They call him: "*Misher Comme-il-faut*".
Respected, honoured, quite at ease.

ROSE: I'll marry Watka; nothing's changed –
Since that's already been arranged.
But weddings here, so it would seem,
Are calculated on what's bid:
The *person* merits scant esteem ...

ORGON: *(With forced laugh.)*
"The person merits scant esteem"!
Come! God forbid! Yes, God forbid!
In this world, things are not so styled
As you imagine them, my child!
Look, in the marriage-market here
No young man bothers to endear
Himself to girls with phrases flowery –
An abstract from his bank-account
Is all he needs to woo a dowry.
Respect for persons doesn't count.
Who you are, none wants to know;
What you *have* is all that matters.
Rich? Then richer still you'll grow:
Poor? For you, it's rags and tatters.
Thousands unite with thousands more;
Millions with millions; fortunes soar
As parents join them, pair by pair:
Heaven or hell, their children's fate –
Depending if they love or hate!
But that comes after – God's affair.

ROSE: I'll marry Watka – more's the pity –
Wealth won't bring me happiness ...

ORGON: *(With increasing bitterness.)*
My dear, if you should chance to meet
Some painted doll, surpassing pretty,
Eyes angelic, nothing less –

Ask her what *she* calls happiness ...
It won't avail you much, my sweet.
"Love and virtue" you'll be told –
But she'll be thinking: "Gold! Gold! Gold!"
What everyone wants is money;
Let the poor wretch who hasn't any
Blush for shame – flee if he can –
The world won't treat him like a man!

ROSE: Dearest Papa, that I should hear
You speak such words! Can that be true?

ORGON: I'm at my wit's end – nothing's clear!
The path before me's normal, straight –
And yet, and yet – I hesitate.
Forward or back, grief must ensue!
Reason forbids me pay attention
To childish whim or apprehension –
But I'm too weak to scorn your tears:
I crave your smile to chase my fears.
In short, whichever way I turn –
Worry or woe – the outlook's bad!

ROSE: *(Kissing his hand, ingratiating, timid.)*
I'm awfully curious to learn
What my dear father thinks of Leon ...

ORGON: Empty-headed, worthless, mad!

ROSE: He only errs through being kind ...

ORGON: Be hanged to that! Whatever cause –
Kindness or lack of discipline –
In my view, sin is always sin.

ROSE: It seems to me, Papa, such flaws
Would disappear; he'd surely alter,
Were he to stand before the altar –
Having chosen as his bride –
A girl, both thrifty and sedate ...

ORGON: Petite – yes? Little upturned nose?

ROSE, confused, lowers her eyes and timidly resumes, after a moment's silence.

ROSE: Papa, you wouldn't …

ORGON: … scold my Rose!
Then be as good as not to state
What you may think his words implied:
He'll have forgotten what he said!

ROSE: "'Twould be his greatest joy to wed".

ORGON: One week's joy, one peaceful year:
Then life-long misery, I fear!

ROSE: True love shared and sound advice …

ORGON: He's penniless! And that won't do
To run a happy home for two:
Forget him! That's *my* sound advice!
Now go!

ROSE: Please …

ORGON: *(Kisses her forehead and turns away.)*
Must I tell you twice?!
(Exit ROSE. ORGON, alone, after a short silence, taps the floor with his stick.)
O world, you villainous old fraud!
Bad faith, dishonour you applaud!
If I could lay my hands on you –
If I could meet you face to face –
I'd set about you with my stick –
I swear I'd beat you black and blue!
"Come on," I'd say, "your answer – quick"
By which do you set greater store:
Cash or conscience? Which counts more?"
I've won no prized, playing fair –
They barely let me up for air!
While cheapjack dandies all look down
And mock the gentry come to town.
Well, let them sneer and let them jeer!

God above sees all things clear:
Whenever there's a job to do,
The dandies squirt you in the eye –
And, quick as loaches, slither by.
The poor old gentry, left to cope,
Unmindful of its rightful due,
A burden bears beyond its scope –
Till sweating blood from every pore …
But what's the use? … I'll say no more!
(Gestures hopelessly and retires to his room.)

SCENE TWO

LEON and PHILIP.

LEON:	Come here a moment – closer, please …
	Come on, still closer, closer still!
	Let's just discuss things at our ease;
	Today I need to talk a bit –
	But, if you lie, one jot or wit –
	I'll dust your hide with such a will,
	Your hair will stand on end with fright!
PHILIP:	You've been off-colour since last night …
LEON:	Who's Watka, tell me, why's his muzzle
	Always sniffing at my heel?
	There's something going on, I feel:
	I sense a mystery – a puzzle!
	How come, we happened to meet here?
	And why his lunatic behaviour?
	All of this, I want made clear
	By you, sir – quickly – do you hear?
PHILIP:	I know nothing, by our Saviour!
LEON:	Come on!
PHILIP:	Sir, I've got to go!
LEON:	For my sake, Philip –

PHILIP: Sorry – no.
                    I'm going …

LEON: *(Grabbing him by the scruff of the neck.)*
                              I'll cut short your route;
                    Head-first, you villain, out you'll fly –
                    That window over there will suit –
                    If you so much as breathe a lie!
                    What were you saying, heart to heart,
                    That time I caught you unaware?
                    Like scalded cats, why did the pair
                    Of you jump guiltily apart?
                    The truth! Or else … !

PHILIP: Yes, sir – I swear!
                    Why should I hide it? There's no need:
                    Pan Watka is himself … Sylphide!

LEON: You rogue!

PHILIP: He's with you everywhere:
                    His cautious hand and watchful eye
                    Safeguard your perpetuity.
                    He's drawing your annuity
                    And he'll be ruined if you die!
                    (Silence.)

LEON: And you?

PHILIP: I've helped him all along,
                    Help was the limit, you perceive,
                    Of my offence – *if* I did wrong!
                    (Silence.)

LEON: The story's easy to believe.
                    So, he was the treacherous ruffian who
                    Enmeshed me in a net so fine
                    I failed to fathom his design
                    Until my last remaining sou.
                    (After a short silence.)
                    But I, too, feel the urge to weave …

	Listen, Philip!
PHILIP:	You were saying?
LEON:	Which shall it be – three ducats net – Or a thrashing that you won't forget?
PHILIP:	The ducats, sir, I can't refuse them …
LEON:	*(Sitting down to write.)* Then find my pistols. Bring them here! Don't dilly-dally!
PHILIP:	I was weighing Whether I ought to, sir … I fear …
LEON:	Go on! I don't intend to use them … *(Exit PHILIP. LEON reads what he has written.)* Having lost you, darling Rose, nothing remains for me, save death. A single shot will still the heart which has always been yours. My pistol is loaded. I wish you happiness and bid you farewell – Leon. *(Folds the note and hands it to PHILIP who has brought the pistols.)* You've betrayed me time and again, So do it now, but cleverly – Here's a letter to Miss Rose – Or Mrs Watka, soon-to-be; As you – so craftily – might suppose It's written with my loving pen; This time, betray with my amen, Give it to Watka –
PHILIP:	Are you sure You've nothing further to command?
LEON:	Nothing. Go! The tip will follow –
PHILIP:	There and back, sir – like a swallow!
	(Exit PHILIP. LEON alone.)
LEON:	What I must do now is ensure My darling Rose knows what I've planned.

(Walks to the door and back.)
But should he suddenly arrive
To find … Old foxes know the ropes!
He might get wind … guess … contrive
To frustrate all my dearest hopes …
No …
(Sitting down.)
    Better write … explain the scheme:
(Writes quickly, then.)
Take heart, my love, it's safe to dream …
(Goes into ROSE's room and quickly reappears.)
Were I to pawn myself and sell
My vigour's last remaining trace –
I cannot – will not – let you fall
Into that Watka's vile embrace!
(Sits down at the right-hand table, with the pistols in front of him.)
Now, features wrought with wild despair,
Hair disordered, eyes distressed –
Let's face our adversary, square …
Here he comes, like one possessed!

Enter WATKA who rushes in and throws himself across the table, covering the pistols.

WATKA:	Murder! Help! Police! Police!
LEON:	What's all this?
WATKA:	Police! Police!
LEON:	Quietly!
WATKA:	I must shout! Haloo!
	Hi, there! Murder!
LEON:	Hold your peace!
	Quiet, or …
WATKA:	Help!
LEON:	*(Sitting, he grabs WATKA by the throat.)*
	I'll strangle you!

WATKA: *(Out of breath.)* Murder! Murder!
(Released, weakening, more quietly.)
> Murder! Murder!

Begins to weep, sob and shake, but remains covering the pistols where he lies across the desk.

LEON: The man's demented, I'm afraid!

WATKA: *(Sobbing.)* No, no! … it's all the … cash I paid …
A huge amount … yes, true – you see …
I purchased … your annuity!

LEON: What harm? …

WATKA: Why? An enormous lot!
You put a bullet through *your* head –
But I'm the one that you'll have shot!
(Springs up and, hiding the pistols, goes and stands on LEON's left, with his back to ORGON's door.)
No … I know what to do instead:
I'll sue! … Your life's my property:
I bought it – it belongs to me!
Since no-one else has any claims;
Whoever dares infringe the same's
A killer, traitor, brigand – further,
He could face a charge of murder!
Murder! Nothing less than murder!
Before the judges I shall kneel,
And your appalling scheme reveal:
How you invoked this criminal measure –
And the gracious court will please
To sentence you to ten years leisure –
Not to mention lawyer's fees!

LEON: Sue if you wish – sue who or whom –
And if you win the case, my friend,
Just post the verdict on my tomb!

WATKA: *(After a short silence.)*
Then, I'll not sue. A shorter way

I'll choose to gain the same self-end:
Philip has gone for the police!

LEON: You must be joking!

WATKA: Then I'll cease!
Once they hear what I've to say,
They will learn that the accused –
As I'll prove convincingly –
Tried to make an end of me:
I've the pistols that you used!

LEON: What of it?

WATKA: Why, you'll be arrested,
Sent to prison!

LEON: For my part,
I promise you, I'll not contest it …
Let them pass sentence, string me up:
No greater joy could fill my cup!

WATKA: *(Confidence shaken, in a low voice.)*
Cross my heart and hope to die!
(Short silence.)
Come, sir, as God is good, why let
Such black despair your soul beset?
Look at the world – so full of gaiety
Look at the clouds, the mountains bold:
Streets and churches, priests and laiety,
Horse-drawn cab and pavement stall –
Great nature's beauteous works behold!
Why yearn to die and leave it all?
Why torture me? I'm poor and old –
Such cruelty nought could justify!
(ORGON and ROSE appear in the background.)
What fault in me can you descry,
That you see fit to persecute
A luckless being such as I?

LEON:	*(As to himself.)*
	My hopes of gaining Rose collapse …
WATKA:	Take her, blast you! She is yours:
	Bullet or wife – same thing perhaps;
	One or the other's bound to cause
	The damned annuity to lapse!
LEON:	I now no longer want a wife –
	I am resolved to take my life!
WATKA:	Dear Leon – gentle, kind and clever!
	Pray do not ruin me forever!
	Leon, my treasure, precious still!
	I'm at your feet – do as you will!
	Trample me! Kick me! Monarch! Lord!
	But, master, one last wish accord:
	If suicide is your intent,
	Then shoot yourself! But if you do,
	Before you die, why not consent –
	I'd gladly raise a cross for you –
	Your death a little to postpone?
	'Twould give you time to start a cure
	With doctors, thermal springs and then,
	Who knows, but the improvement shown
	Might give you courage to endure?
	With roses in your cheeks again,
	A buyer might well feel inspired …
	I wouldn't raise the price at all;
	You're done for once the shot is fired,
	But why should I go to the wall … ?
	Leon, my jewel, pity me!
	Salvage my annuity!
	It's no great service I request –
	You've all eternity to rest!
	Six more months on earth with us
	Won't ruin al that's left! Why fuss?

LEON:	Must make an end of it today …
WATKA:	They you, yourself, redeem it! Pay …
	A modest sum … a trifle, what?
	Give me back half! A teeny slice …
	(Weeping.)
	And I, myself, will fire the shot!
LEON:	I'm broke!
WATKA:	An hour from now suffice?
LEON:	Not even ten …
WATKA:	Perhaps a year?
	A mortgage of some sort would do …
LEON:	I haven't one.
WATKA:	You've got … Silbeed,
	Yes?

WATKA had misheard and misunderstood "Sylphide", which he took to be a property owned by LEON.

LEON:	Don't mock!
WATKA:	As if I'd jeer!
	Who'd mock you in such urgent need?
	Give me your word!

ORGON makes a sign to LEON to give his word.

LEON:	I give my word …
WATKA:	You'll pay me half?
LEON:	A year from now …
WATKA:	Then that's agreed, as you've all heard.
	No hanky-panky?
LEON:	Cross my heart!
	But where is *your* security?
WATKA:	*(Handing over papers.)*
	Take these papers for a start …
	You'll not play monkey tricks, you swear?
LEON:	I'd treasure life beyond compare,

	With such a girl my wife-to-be!
	You'll grant me Rose's hand, Orgon?
ORGON:	He did *say* you could take her, true!
LEON:	But how say you, Rose?
ROSE:	Oh, Leon!
	My life … my life, I owe to you!
LEON:	*(Pointing to WATKA.)*

Let's not forget to thank our friend
Who snatched the pistols from my hand!
I hadn't loaded them, it's true –
But how on earth was he to tell?
For making sure all ended well –
And for enabling me to wed
Rose, who will care for me instead;
For Watka's change of heart, praise be –
(Waving the deed given him by WATKA.)
And long live my annuity!

*While LEON declaims "Life would be sweet beyond compare"
etc., WATKA has been creeping towards a chair where he
stands in a daze until, with the last line, he slumps helplessly
into the seat.*

THE END